The Decline of Industrial Britain 1870–1980

HISTORICAL CONNECTIONS
Series editors
David Blackbourn, Birkbeck College, University of London
Geoffrey Crossick, University of Essex
John Davis, University of Warwick
Joanna Innes, Somerville College, University of Oxford

The Decline of Industrial Britain 1870–1980

Michael Dintenfass

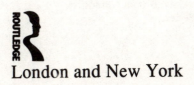

London and New York

First published 1992
by Routledge
11 New Fetter Lane, London EC4P 4EE

Simultaneously published in the USA and Canada by
Routledge
a division of Routledge, Chapman and Hall, Inc.
29 West 35th Street, New York, NY 10001

Typeset in 10/12pt Times by
Ponting-Green Publishing Services, Sunninghill, Berks
Printed in Great Britain by
Clays Ltd, St Ives plc

British Library Cataloguing in Publication Data
Dintenfass, Michael
  Decline of Industrial Britain, 1870–1980
  I. Title
  330.9415

Library of Congress Cataloging in Publication Data
Dintenfass, Michael,
  The decline of industrial Britain, 1870–1980 / Michael Dintenfass.
       p.   cm. – (Historical connections)
  Includes bibliographical references (p.   ) and index
  1. Great Britain – Economic conditions – 19th century. 2. Great
  Britain – Economic conditions – 20th century. 3. Great Britain –
  Industries – History – 19th century. 4. Great Britain – Industries –
  History – 20th century.   I. Title   Series.
  HC255.D56   1992
  338–0941   dc20   91–47996

ISBN 0-415-05465-6

To the former Prime Minister,
she so enriched the subject

Contents

Series editors' preface

Historical Connections is a new series of short books on important historical topics and debates, written primarily for those studying and teaching history. The books will offer original and challenging works of synthesis that will make new themes accessible, or old themes accessible in new ways, build bridges between different chronological periods and different historical debates, and encourage comparative discussion in history.

If the study of history is to remain exciting and creative, then the tendency to fragmentation must be resisted. The inflexibility of older assumptions about the relationship between economic, social, cultural and political history has been exposed by recent historical writing, but the impression has sometimes been left that history is little more than a chapter of accidents. This series will insist on the importance of processes of historical change, and it will explore the connections within history: connections between different layers and forms of historical experience, as well as connections that resist the fragmentary consequences of new forms of specialism in historical research.

Historical Connections will put the search for these connections back at the top of the agenda by exploring new ways of uniting the different strands of historical experience, and by affirming the importance of studying change and movement in history.

David Blackbourn
Geoffrey Crossick
John Davis
Joanna Innes

Acknowledgments

Peter Marsh gave me the courage to write this book, and John Davis gave me the opportunity. I am indebted to them both. At the University of Wisconsin-Milwaukee, Ron Ross brought enlightenment to numerous conversations about British manufacturing, and Bruce Fetter took time from his manifold commitments to read the manuscript. I am also grateful to Bob Moeller and to the editors of the Historical Connections series for their comments about this work. Fred Dintenfass, Willy Dintenfass, and Lucy Morris all took turns at my keyboard. Readers of this book will want to watch out for their publications.

Portions of this book were composed in the midst of the most serious personal difficulties, and I would like to thank my friend Richard Kaiser for an emotional solidarity that made work possible and which the word friendship does not begin to describe.

Above all, I am grateful to Polly Morris. She always insisted that I find the best in myself and sustained my efforts with all the precious gifts at her disposal. If I have not succeeded here, that is my responsibility alone.

Milwaukee
October 1991

Introduction

The average Briton of 1870 was almost certainly wealthier than the ordinary citizen of every other country at that moment in history. His descendants in the 1980s were incomparably richer than he had been. Gross domestic product per person (adjusted for inflation) increased more than threefold just between 1900 and 1984. The accompanying rise in disposable income allowed the ordinary British household to purchase a more extensive and more varied array of goods and services.

In the 1880s food dominated private consumption in Britain, accounting for one-third of all consumer expenditure and for between one-half and two-thirds of the expenses of wage-earning families. A century later, dietary requirements (themselves now more heavily weighted in favour of meat, dairy products, and fresh fruits and vegetables) claimed only 15 per cent of all consumer expenditure and a mere one-fifth of the average family budget. By the 1980s the overwhelming majority of British households had money available for the acquisition of expensive domestic appliances. Ninety-five per cent of all households had refrigerators in 1985 and 82 per cent had washing machines. Ninety-seven per cent of British households possessed televisions; indeed 86 per cent possessed color televisions. By contrast, the new consumer durable of the late nineteenth century – the bicycle – remained a luxury item until after the turn of the century; its use even in the 1880s and 1890s was confined largely to the middle classes at their leisure. Increased wealth led to wider horizons as well as more extensive possessions. Seventeen million Britons took holidays abroad in 1986 – virtually 30 per cent of the population. Finally, infant mortality – that most sensitive indicator of a people's welfare – fell dramatically as wealth multiplied in Britain: from 153 deaths per 1,000 live births in the 1890s to 12.04 deaths in 1980 and 9.4 in 1985.

Unlike his ancestors a century before, the average Briton of the 1980s no longer represented the standard of affluence to which the inhabitants of other lands aspired. In thirteen of the twenty-four countries of the Organisation for Economic Co-operation and Development (OECD) the level of Gross Domestic Product (GDP) per person attained in 1987 surpassed that of the United Kingdom. The United States, Germany, Japan, and France had all moved ahead of Britain in terms of GDP per capita since 1870. So too had Finland, Iceland, and Norway. In fourteen of the OECD countries there were more passenger cars per 1,000 inhabitants in the mid-1980s than in Britain, and in nine there were more television sets. More infants died before the age of 12 months (per 1,000 live births) in Britain in 1985 than in fifteen other OECD countries, including such economic dynamos as Ireland and Spain.[1]

Since 1870 each succeeding generation of Britons has achieved a material standard of living that would have been unimaginable to its parents when children. Yet the rapid increase in the wealth of the inhabitants of the British Isles has not been nearly so dramatic as the increases in wealth experienced in western Europe, North America, and Japan. Herein lies the essence of Britain's economic performance since 1870: while the economy has proven ever more successful at generating wealth, the absolute increase in the British production of goods and services has been *relatively* slow compared to that achieved elsewhere. The consequence of this relative decline has been that Britain has lost its place at the top of the league table for wealth per individual and has tumbled to a middle ranking among industrial economies, roughly on a par with Italy.

Britain's relative economic decline – its causes and the remedies for them – has occasioned a great deal of academic interest, and the disputes among the professors will supply much of the raw material for this book. But Britain's decline has not been merely an academic matter. Competing responses to the country's relative economic failure have shaped British politics, from Joseph Chamberlain's campaign for tariff reform in 1903 and Lloyd George's Keynesian program of 1929, to Harold Wilson's enthusiasm for government planning and technological innovation in the 1960s, and Margaret Thatcher's bid to restore market forces and the incentive of private enrichment to their rightful place in British culture in our own day. The management of the economy has been a major determinant of the fortunes of British governments, and their policies have tested, albeit imperfectly, the accuracy of the different diagnoses of the 'British disease' and the responsiveness of the patient to the various therapies on offer.

The attempts to reverse Britain's relative economic decline have managed only the most modest success thus far. British growth rates after the severe recession of the early 1980s exceeded those of her competitors, but substantial gaps in efficiency and wealth-creating power remain. With the trade balance showing deficits of historic dimensions and the inflation rate in Britain once again rising faster than elsewhere, the fear grows that the great leap forward of the middle and late 1980s was a one-off affair that cannot be sustained.

In the light of these considerations, the critical examination of the causes of Britain's relatively poor economic performance since 1870 cannot be simply a tour of the past undertaken out of intellectual curiosity. It is inevitably also an inquest on the present and perhaps a guide to the future.

1 The historical record

The shape of the British economy changed substantially after 1870. Resources were reallocated among agriculture, industry, and services, and the contribution of each sector to employment and output was altered. Within industry the trades of the first industrial revolution declined in importance, and the manufactures based upon late-nineteenth-century and twentieth-century advances in chemistry and physics came to the fore. Large corporations multiplied in number and acquired considerable power throughout the economy. How did British developments compare with the structural changes taking place in other industrialized countries? What does the comparison tell us about Britain's relative economic decline?

The British economy of 1870 was already recognizable as an industrial economy. Agriculture, the mainstay of economic life everywhere for centuries, was the smallest sector of the economy, accounting for less than one-quarter of employment and less than one-sixth of gross domestic product. A century after the mechanization of spinning in the then small and unimportant cotton textile industry, manufacturing had grown to a prominent place in the nation's economy. Representing 42 per cent of employment and 40 per cent of production, industry was roughly twice as important as agriculture. Services accounted for the single largest share of output (45 per cent), but the tertiary sector did not yet employ as many workers as industry (Mitchell 1978: 433; and Maddison 1982: 205).

The next century saw the continuation of those trends that had been at work between 1780 and 1870. The decline of agriculture accelerated, and by 1970 farming accounted for only one-fiftieth of Britain's workers and for about the same proportion of national output. Services monopolized the resources released from the primary sector, and their share of both output and employment increased to about 60 per cent. Industry's role in the economy remained more or less constant, employment and production in this sector falling only a few percentage points between 1870 and 1970 (Mitchell 1978: 433; and Maddison 1982: 205).[2]

The relatively stable position of industry in the economy masks the fundamental changes that occurred within this sector after 1870. The composition of manufacturing activity in late-nineteenth-century Britain reflected the fabric- and mineral-intensive nature of the initial phase of British industrialization. Textiles and clothing manufacture accounted for 41 per cent of the industrial labor force in 1871, and the nation's miners represented an additional 9 per cent (Mitchell and Deane 1962: 60). These same industries also dominated Britain's overseas trade. Exports of cottons, woolens, linen, and silk, and coal, coke, and related products made up virtually 60 per cent of Britain's commodity trade in 1870 (Deane and Cole 1967: 31).

By the 1950s and 1960s cloth and coal no longer formed the foundation of Britain's industrial sector. Together they claimed only 17 per cent of the manufacturing work-force in 1965, and their combined share of British commodity exports had already fallen to less than one-quarter by 1950 (Mitchell and Jones 1971: 41–2; and Deane and Cole 1967: 31). Now British manufacturing was metal- and appliance-intensive. Four out of every ten industrial workers (male and female) in Britain in 1965 were employed producing metals and assembling appliances. Engineering and the production of electrical goods claimed almost one worker in five and vehicle manufacture another 7 per cent. Ninety-five years earlier metal-working, in all its manifold varieties, had provided work for only one out of six British workers (Mitchell and Deane 1962: 60; and Mitchell and Jones 1971: 41–2). Export figures also registered the displacement of textiles and coal by engineering. Between 1870 and 1950 machinery and vehicle exports increased from one-fiftieth of British overseas sales to fully one-third (Deane and Cole 1967: 31).

Noteworthy changes in the importance of various lesser industries also marked British economic developments after 1870. The food, drink, and tobacco industries – the sixth largest employer of labor in 1871 – experienced a 25 per cent reduction in their share of the manufacturing work-force to 1965. Chemicals, by contrast, increased its share of industrial employment almost fourfold over the same period, and paper, printing, and publishing increased their share more than twofold – though in both cases rapid growth proceeded from a small base (Mitchell and Deane 1962: 60; and Mitchell and Jones 1971: 41–2). The chemicals industry also experienced an eightfold increase in its share of British exports (Deane and Cole 1967: 31).

As the allocation of resources among agriculture, industry, and services and within manufacturing changed, British enterprises grew in size, and the structures of individual industries lost their atomistic character. In the late nineteenth century employment and market share in most branches of the economy were spread over a large number of concerns. Individual enterprises attained considerable size, but they accounted for only a minor share of the trade in their industry; their rivals remained numerous, and relations among them were highly competitive. In the course of the next century there emerged in many sectors individual concerns that claimed shares of employment and sales large enough to enable them to exercise considerable influence over rival traders. In short, industry became concentrated.

Already in 1930 the five largest firms accounted for 70 per cent or more of the trade in eight of fifteen principal industrial categories in Britain, including food, tobacco, chemicals, shipbuilding, paper and publishing, building materials, miscellaneous metal goods, and miscellaneous manufacturing. Only in drink (41 per cent) and metal manufacture (46 per cent) did the five biggest firms account for less than half of total business (Hannah 1976: 225). Forty years on, the dominance of large corporations was one of the fundamental facts of economic life in Britain. The 100 largest manufacturing concerns (measured by sales) in 1970 accounted for approximately 60 per cent of the total net assets of domestic manufacturing industry, 45 per cent of the work-force, and 60 per cent of total sales (Channon 1973:17). Small firms, meanwhile, were fast disappearing. There were 76,000 fewer companies employing 200 people or less in 1963 than there had been in 1935, and their combined share of manufacturing output was a mere 16 per cent (Hannah 1976a: 1). If competition continued to characterize British industry late in the twentieth century, it was the oligopolistic competition of a few large corporations and not the atomistic competition of numerous small firms that had defined the marketplace in 1870.

Though the British economy of 1980 was significantly different from that of 1870, the 1980 economy had far more in common with other developed economies than had been the case in the late nineteenth century. Of the economies of western Europe, North America, and Japan in 1871, only Britain's had assumed a distinctly industrial character. Elsewhere agriculture still accounted for half or more of the work-force (France and Germany 49 per cent, the USA 50 per cent, Italy 62 per cent, and Japan 72 per cent), and for between 22 and 60 per cent of national product (the USA 22 per cent, Germany 40 per cent,

France 43 per cent, and Italy 57 per cent) (Maddison 1982: 205; Mitchell 1978: 426–33; and Davis *et al.* 1972: 55).

After 1870 the countries of western Europe and North America and Japan rapidly directed resources away from farming, and as they did so their economies came to resemble the British economy in structure. By 1970 agriculture's share of total output had fallen to 10 per cent or less not just in Britain but also in the United States, France, Germany, Italy, Japan, and the Netherlands. If farming's share of output in Britain (2 per cent) was smaller than elsewhere, its place in the German economy (3 per cent) was only slightly larger. Industry, which had accounted for 40 per cent of production in Britain in 1870 but less than 30 per cent elsewhere, now represented between 29.5 per cent (the USA) and 54 per cent (Germany) of the output of the advanced industrial economies. While industry accounted for a somewhat smaller share of production in Britain than in Germany, France, and Italy, industry's contribution to the British economy was considerably larger than its contribution to the American economy. Finally, the service sector was now the single largest source of output in the United States, Japan, Italy, and the Netherlands as well as in Britain (Mitchell 1978: 426–33; Davis *et al.* 1972: 55; and Ohkawa and Rosovsky 1973: 284–5).[3]

This broad convergence in the basic structures of the developed economies was paralleled by a similar process of convergence within the industrial sector. In continental Europe and North America metal manufacture and engineering came to dominate industrial activity as they did in Britain. At the turn of the century food, drink, and tobacco production combined with the textile industries to supply some 40–50 per cent of the manufacturing output of the industrial economies (OEEC countries 50 per cent, UK 43 per cent, and the USA 44 per cent). Metal products (excluding basic metals) accounted for 10–16 per cent of output, and chemicals contributed 5–6 per cent. By 1959 this pattern of industrial activity had been reversed. Metal goods and chemicals now accounted for half or more of all industrial production (OEEC countries 50 per cent, UK 51 per cent, and the USA 56 per cent), and food, drink and tobacco and textiles produced only 19–20 per cent of manufacturing output (Maizels 1963: 46). The composition of manufacturing employment changed in a similar fashion, and the result was a nearly identical distribution of industrial work-forces in the developed economies, as Table 1, showing German and British manufacturing employment in 1970, demonstrates (O. T. Jones 1976: 79):

Table 1

	Food and drink	Textiles and clothing	Chemicals
UK	10%	14%	9%
Germany	10%	13%	10%
	Basic metals	Metal products	Other
UK	7%	44%	16%
Germany	5%	46%	17%

Britain's shift toward a machine-based export trade after 1870 was also part of a larger trend in 'world' trade.[4] In 1899 textiles and apparel made up 40 per cent of the trade in manufactured goods among the countries of North America and western Europe, India, and Japan, and engineering wares just less than 20 per cent. Half a century later the positions of these industries were almost exactly the opposite of what they had been, metal manufactures and electrical goods accounting for 44 per cent of international commodity exchange, and textiles and clothing for about 20 per cent (Tyszynski 1951: 283). Britain's pattern of trade specialization after 1870 was thus clearly of a piece with the specializations of other industrialized economies.

If the emergence of an increasingly service-based economy and an appliance-orientated industry defined Britain's resemblance to other industrial nations, so too did the transition from a competitive economy to a corporate economy. The tendency toward large-scale enterprise and industrial concentration was apparent in all the advanced economies in the period 1870–1980, and the pacemaker in this regard was not Britain but the United States. The American economy began to evolve in the direction of big corporations and oligopoly in the decades after the Civil War, and by 1909 industrial concentration in the United States was considerably greater than in Britain (Chandler 1980b; and Hannah 1980: 42). German business likewise showed a marked propensity to greater size and concentrated market power after unification, though it is not clear that change was more rapid than in Britain (Kocka 1980: 105).

Any British lag in the transition to the corporate economy, however, was short-lived. By the mid-1920s the country's 100 largest industrial firms accounted for about the same share of manufacturing output (roughly 22 per cent) as did the 100 largest American companies. The output shares of the respective top 100s fluctuated over the next three decades, but they did so in tandem and remained comparable. From the

1950s the tendency to size and concentration accelerated in Britain. By the 1970s Britain possessed the most concentrated industrial structure among developed economies; the share of net manufacturing output produced by the 100 largest concerns (43 per cent) was 30 per cent greater than the share of the 100 largest industrial firms in the United States, the country with the second most concentrated manufacturing sector (Hannah 1980: 42 and 71). Britain's greatest corporations were now international giants. Fifty British companies employed 20,000 or more employees in 1973, 12.5 per cent of the world total of such corporations. If the United States could boast many more such industrial behemoths, Britain's tally far exceeded those of Germany (29), Japan (28), and France (24) (McCraw 1988: 478). However hesitant may have been its start, Britain developed into a corporate economy *par excellence*.

In the century after 1870 the developed industrial economies of western Europe, North America, and Japan came to resemble the British economy ever more closely. In all of these countries agriculture was supplanted as the biggest sector of the economy, industry assumed an important role, and services garnered an ever-growing share of output and employment. Metal goods, chemicals, and electrical and electronic appliances displaced textiles and food and drink as the key manufacturing industries, and large firms and oligopolistic competition became the defining features of the marketplace. In no fundamental respect did the structure of the British economy differ significantly from the structures of other industrial economies.

Yet the greater the structural similarity between Britain's economy and the economies of Germany, France, Italy, Japan, and the United States, the less able were British producers to compete effectively with their western European, North American, and Japanese rivals. The more Britain and her competitors concentrated resources upon the same tasks and the more these tasks were concentrated in the hands of large corporations, the weaker was Britain's grasp upon the export markets of the world *and* the domestic markets of Britain itself.

As late as the turn of the century Britain still accounted for almost one-third of the total 'world' trade in manufactured goods. This was half as large again as Germany's share and three times the share of the United States (Tyszynski 1951: 286). Seventy-five years later Britain's share of the world trade in industrial commodities had fallen to less than one-tenth, and Britain now ranked behind the United States, Germany, Japan, and France as a trading nation (Brown and Sheriff 1979: 241). The changes in the composition of world trade that occurred in these decades were scarcely more unfavorable to Britain than to its principal competitors (Tyszynski 1951: 288–92; and Alford 1988: 43–4). Rather it was Britain's inability to keep pace in precisely those markets in which it was well placed to do business that was at the root of the deterioration in Britain's export position.

Britain's recent performance in the markets for technology-intensive products illustrates all too graphically this inability to compete in industries where its economy suffered no inherent disadvantages. The goods in question were commodities that Britain ought to have been able to produce and sell on a competitive basis. They required only small inputs of those resources with which Britain was poorly endowed – natural resources and cheap labor – but embodied the knowledge and technical skill that ought to have been abundantly accessible to an affluent country like Britain. Yet the record has been one of declining competitiveness. Britain's share of the international trade in research-based industries fell from 12 to 8.5 per cent between 1964 and 1984, and in 1985 the economy recorded a deficit of £2.5 billion in the trade of information technology (Jenkins 1988: 275–6). Nor has Britain done any better in the provision of those private services – freight, insurance, and transportation – in which it once held a commanding position but whose efficiency increasingly has depended upon the utilization of information technology. In just twenty-one years Britain's stake in the international trade of private services fell by more than 40 per cent to only 15 per cent in 1976 (Brown and Sheriff 1979: 246).

In recent years the displacement of British producers from their home markets has matched the long-term decline in their ability to compete for exports. Foreign manufacturers increased their stake in the British market for industrial products from 11 per cent in 1961 to 28 per cent in 1975 (Alford 1988: 42). By the early 1980s British imports of manufactured goods exceeded British exports – reversing a positive balance that had persisted since the industrial revolution. This penetration of foreign products into British homes and workplaces has been a broad-based phenomenon extending across a wide range of manufactures. A study by the Department of Trade and Industry showed that sixteen of twenty-one broadly defined industrial categories recorded trade deficits in 1984 – including such pivotal trades as motor manufacture, office equipment and data-processing machinery, electrical and electronic engineering, and instrument manufacture. Moreover, foreign goods now accounted for 30 per cent or more of domestic sales in sixteen industries, including, in addition to those just listed, chemicals, man-made fibres, mechanical engineering, and 'other transport' – all industries where British exports still exceeded imports (House of Lords 1985: 17–19).

Since 1870 the British economy has used the basic factors of production in much the same ways as the economies of the United States, Japan, Germany, Italy, and France but without achieving a comparable return on its investment. Britain's problem, evidently, is not that it has misallocated the land, labor, and capital available to it. It is that it has failed to employ these resources as productively as other economies in performing the same mix of economic activities. Why?

The following chapters will explore various hypotheses concerning Britain's inability to make as much as other countries out of the same lines of business in an effort to come to an understanding of the "British disease."

2 Tools and techniques

Most British equipment is in use twenty years after it should have been scrapped. It is because you keep this used-up machinery that the US is making you a back number.

Andrew Carnegie

Assuming the right machinery is installed and the right technical knowledge is possessed by the management, I have yet to find a single case in any industry in which Britain cannot compete satisfactorily with Germany, Czechoslovakia or Japan.

Isaac M. Sieff

The failure of manufacturers to replace the tools and techniques that vaulted Britain to international pre-eminence after 1770 with the more efficient production methods that became available in the late nineteenth century and in the twentieth has probably been the most frequently invoked explanation of the nation's failure to remain competitive with the industrial economies of western Europe, North America, and Japan. Certainly technological backwardness is the most venerable explanation of the "British disease." The first such charges were voiced long before there was any suspicion of decline. Moreover, this resistance to innovations in machinery and production methods has been alleged against entrepreneurs in a wide range of industries. Managers in industries dependent upon the technologies of electricity and steel have been condemned along with those in industries that were dependent upon steam and iron; those manufacturing producers' goods have been indicted along with those manufacturing consumer goods.

The original complaints about the indifference of British industrialists to new developments in production techniques appeared when Britain was still the undisputed "Workshop of the World." Already in the mid-1850s the Committee on the Machinery of the United States warned that American machine builders would penetrate the British market if domestic producers showed "a want of energy in improving their machinery." The official *Report on the Paris Universal Exhibition, 1867* described a woolen and worsted industry that was lagging behind its overseas rivals in the introduction of new techniques, and in 1884 the engineer Charles Siemens charged that "the English engineering employer took 'less interest in the technical part of his work than either a German or a French employer' and was more prejudiced against innovation than his foreign counterparts." Such laments continued past the turn of the century and through the First World War. In 1903 a Yorkshire coalmaster conceded that he and his fellow mine owners were "slow in making new departures." In 1917 no less a figure than the president of the Institute of Mechanical Engineers spoke critically "about the ill-planned and ill-equipped engineering shops" (Coleman and MacLeod 1986: 589–92).

The claim that British businessmen have preferred antiquated tools and techniques to newer, more productive practices has remained a dominant theme of twentieth-century commentary upon Britain's economic ills. In 1929 a firm of American consultants observed that the blast furnaces employed in the Scottish section of the iron and steel industry were not "adapted in design or capacity to present day conditions of competitive iron manufacture." Twenty years later another team of American observers reported on the cotton industry's "reluctance to depart from things past" and noted the "iron-clad arguments against re-equipment" that came forth from Lancashire (ibid.: 589–91). Such criticisms provided the raw materials out of which economic historians like David S. Landes, Derek H. Aldcroft, and A.L. Levine fashioned their accounts of Britain's industrial decline in the 1950s and 1960s. Similar complaints can still be heard today. The House of Lords Select Committee appointed to "consider the causes and implications of the deficit in the United Kingdom's balance of trade in manufactures" reported in 1985 – one hundred and thirty years after the Committee on the Machinery of the United States published its findings – that Britain's "capital is relatively older and incorporates less new technology than that of its competitors" (House of Lords 1985: 25).

As these examples indicate, those critical of British entrepreneurship found signs of technological conservatism in a disturbingly broad array of industries. If the old staple trades – coal, textiles, iron and steel, and engineering – persisted with antiquated production methods, so too did newer industries such as chemicals, electricity supply, and electrical appliances and electronics, even after the development of high-speed, high-volume repetition methods in the bicycle and boot-and-shoe industries of Britain. Nor did the nature of the finished product provide much immunity against this disease. Capital-goods industries, including tinplate and machine tools, succumbed to the sclerosis of technique, and so did pottery and printing, sectors supplying the consuming public directly (Coleman and MacLeod 1986: 589–95).

The larger implications of this peculiarly British aversion to innovation were not lost on those who identified the resistance of British entrepreneurs to new methods and machines. Old-fashioned equipment, they argued, was the fundamental cause of lost trade, slow growth, and unemployment. Arnold Toynbee, discoursing on "the idolization of ephemeral technique" and "the breakdowns of civilizations" in his *A Study of History*, declared that "in our day the country that gave birth to the Industrial System of production is a by-word for its technological conservatism." "And the seriousness of the handicap," he concluded, could "be gauged by the plight in which our British industry finds itself to-day" (Toynbee 1939: 428–30).

Much of the material from which this portrait of complacency and conservatism was drawn was of doubtful validity. Witnesses before official committees had their own views and interests to promote, and it was easy to mistake short-term trends for long-term developments. Even the most objective analysts might unwittingly make do with an inadequate sample or fail to distinguish the exceptional from the typical. What is perhaps most striking in retrospect is how much of this discussion of the failings of British industrialists in the area of technical choice proceeded without any serious consideration of those innovations that were introduced in British manufacturing.

When all of the qualifications have been made, however, the fact remains that there is something in the charge of excessive technological conservatism. A significant number of British industries – indeed a number of Britain's most significant industries – did trail behind their overseas competitors in the adoption of new production practices and the new products that came with them. In the middle 1930s almost half the coal mined in Britain was still cut by hand even though machines now accounted for more than nine-tenths of all the coal mined in Germany, Belgium, and France (Buxton 1979: 60–1). Sixty-five years earlier British chemical producers had chosen to continue with the Leblanc method of making soda even though the superiority of the Solvay process had been demonstrated and continental and American firms were adopting the latter technique. Similarly domestic firms neglected Sir William Perkin's pioneering work in the production of synthetic dyes and so allowed Germany to achieve a virtual monopoly over a market that was largely British (Landes 1969: 272–4; Aldcroft and Richardson 1969: 147; and Sandberg 1981: 112–14).

By 1913 German and American imports dominated the British market for electrical machinery and electric lamps, while British manufacturers were left with the trade in less sophisticated electrical products (mainly cables) – and Britain's uncompetitiveness in this industry derived from the hesitant response of domestic industrialists to technological changes in the provision of power and light and the chaotic development of electricity supply (Byatt 1968). Even the construction industry exhibited a pronounced resistance to changes in methods and products. Britain's first substantial steel-framed building was erected two decades after the pioneering American project. The regular use of those techniques of prefabrication that had been introduced at the Crystal Palace exhibition of 1851 was long delayed, and reinforced concrete and mechanization were adopted quite slowly (Coleman and MacLeod 1986: 583–4).

Figures comparing productivity growth in Britain and other industrial economies suggest that coal, chemicals, construction, and the electrical-goods industry were part of a larger pattern of technological backwardness and not isolated exceptions to a more progressive tendency. Labor productivity (gross domestic product per hour worked) increased more slowly in Britain than in Japan, Sweden, France, Italy, Germany, Belgium, the Netherlands, and the United States over the period 1870–1984 (Feinstein 1988: 5, Table 2). Multifactor productivity (the measure of the efficiency with which labor and capital are combined for productive purposes) grew more slowly in Britain between 1950 and 1973 than in the Netherlands, Germany, Japan, and France. Indeed, in the Netherlands, where multifactor productivity rose at a slower rate than in Germany, Japan, and France, the pace of productivity advance was more than half again as rapid as in Britain (ibid.: 11, Table 4).

These statistics, like the qualitative evidence introduced above, do not provide conclusive proof that British entrepreneurs habitually neglected the most efficient technologies. Labor productivity may have grown comparatively slowly in Britain because workers there were less skilled or less industrious. The observed disparity in the rate of increase in multifactor productivity could have been a function of an inefficient allocation of resources among the various branches of the economy, a marked superiority in British technique and productivity at the start of the period of measurement, or an unequal capacity to exploit the same technologies with a similar degree of effectiveness. None the less these data on comparative productivity growth do not exonerate British industrialists of the charge of technological conservatism, and together with the more impressionistic evidence of British backwardness they form a case that requires serious examination.

In order to judge the responsiveness of manufacturers in Britain to innovations in machines and methods it is necessary to investigate specific cases of technological choice in industries that were at the center of the economy. Here we shall concentrate on iron and steel, cotton textiles, and motor cars. In each case a once highly competitive and profitable industry experienced a precipitous decline. In each case British companies eschewed production techniques that found wide-spread employment in other countries. Iron and steel, cotton, and automobiles – the worst single instances of industrial failure in the late nineteenth century, the inter-war period, and the 1970s and 1980s respectively – all would seem to exemplify the technological origins of Britain's economic decline. But is the appearance an accurate guide to the underlying reality? Did entrepreneurs in these trades undermine the efficiency and prosperity of their firms by failing to modernize their tools and techniques? Or was it that British conditions differed from those abroad and in ways that made the abandonment of inherited practices uneconomic?

The dominance over the international trade in basic metals that British iron and steel firms secured in the course of the industrial revolution persisted through the third quarter of the nineteenth century. In 1875–9 Britain still produced 46 per cent of the world's pig iron and 36 per cent of its steel. British producers enjoyed a near monopoly over the domestic market (96 per cent of British iron and steel consumption in 1876–85 was produced at home), and they supplied almost three-quarters (73 per cent) of the iron and steel that entered into international trade (Sandberg 1981: 107; and McCloskey 1973: 42).

Over the next four decades Britain's lead in the production of basic metals was lost. Germany and the United States both surpassed Britain in the output of iron and steel, and by the eve of the First World War Britain's share of international production had fallen to 14 per cent for pig iron and 10 per cent for steel. More serious still, Britain's grip on the iron and steel trade slackened considerably. Its share of iron and steel exports fell to only 34 per cent in 1904–13, and Germany now claimed the first position among metal-trading nations. Finally, foreign producers (principally German companies) made serious inroads into the British market, their share of British consumption rising to 22 per cent in the period 1904–13 (Sandberg 1981: 107; McCloskey 1973: 42; and Elbaum 1986: 51).

This dramatic decline in Britain's standing as an iron and steel producer coincided with major departures in the technology of metal-making and the manifestly slow diffusion of these innovations among British concerns. In the late 1870s the Thomas–Gilchrist "basic" process for making steel was invented in Britain. A technique for removing "embrittling phosphorous from pig iron," the Thomas–Gilchrist technique opened the way to the utilization of the abundant phosphorous-rich ores in the production of steel. By the late 1880s basic steelmaking had come to predominate among continental steel companies. Its adoption in Britain, however, was much less rapid, and basic steelmaking would supplant acid steelmaking there only in the 1930s (McCloskey 1973: 57).

The last decades of the nineteenth century also saw significant changes in the operation of blast furnaces. Hotter blasts at greater pressures, the connection of individual furnaces to separate blowing engines, improvements in engine design, the mechanical charging of furnaces, and systems for the delivery of hot metal to steelworks – all these enhanced the efficiency of pig iron production. While there was no necessary connection between these innovations and the Thomas–Gilchrist process, the erection of facilities for making basic steel provided iron and steel companies with the opportunity to modernize the operation of their blast furnaces. The persistence of British firms with acid steelmaking thus curtailed innovations in the production of pig iron (Allen 1981: 42–51).

The British iron and steel industry as a whole showed a marked indifference to the Thomas–Gilchrist process and to the new developments in blast-furnace practice at the very time that its competitive advantage over Germany and the United States was fast slipping away. It is not necessarily the case, however, that the industry's managers were acting irrationally in limiting their adoption of the new techniques. If the demand for British iron and steel was stagnant or growing only very slowly, if the resource requirements of the new methods were prohibitively expensive, or if the efficiency of the established plant was sufficiently high that the net gain from the new methods would not have significantly improved the performance of their enterprises, then the ironmasters would have been justified in their choice of technique. The key question is whether any of these conditions obtained in the late Victorian and Edwardian iron and steel industry.

The demand for iron and steel undoubtedly grew more slowly in Britain than in Germany or the United States in this period, but an increase of 3.4 per cent per annum between 1890 and 1913 certainly was large enough to warrant new investment in the industry. Moreover, the demand for ship-plate, tinplate, and sheet – high quality products in the manufacture of which basic open-hearth steel had an undisputed advantage – grew faster still. Historians of the iron and steel industry have not doubted that the "aggregate demand expansion for British steel . . . was more than sufficient to permit the establishment of entirely new, integrated facilities at greenfield sites"; and the construction of at least "a dozen American-style blast furnaces . . . as part of integrated plants to make basic steel" in the Cleveland district of north-east England between 1900 and 1914 would appear to confirm their judgment (Elbaum 1986: 57–8 and 73–4; and Allen 1979: 937). Consequently there seems no reason to believe that the size of the market inhibited the further utilization of the new methods of making iron and steel.

Nor is it likely that input costs retarded the expansion of basic steelmaking in Britain and the modernization of blast-furnace operations. The phosphorous-rich ores that the Thomas–Gilchrist process made usable were exactly the ores with which Britain was well endowed. In fact the highly phosphoric ironstone of the north-east provided the cheapest iron ore in the world. Technical difficulties thwarted its exploitation before 1890, but thereafter mixing machines and the Talbot tilting open-hearth furnace made possible the production of steel from Cleveland ores at costs as low as any German or American producer could achieve (Allen 1979: 929 and 935–7). The ironstone of the East Midlands was also suitable for basic steelmaking. If it was uneconomical to locate Thomas–Gilchrist works near these ore deposits (owing to their distance from the consumers of steel), it does not seem to have been prohibitively expensive to ship the ore to steelmakers on the north-east coast (Elbaum 1986: 72 and 78; and Payne 1968: 90). In any event, Britain suffered no comparative disadvantage as far as supplies of ore were concerned. Germany, Britain's principal competitor in the iron and steel trade, managed to develop basic steelmaking on a large scale despite the fact that it lacked suitable ore in sufficient quantity and had to import it from Sweden (Elbaum 1986: 71–3; and Allen 1979: 929 and 935).

The enduring attachment of British iron and steel companies to plant that was laid down when acid steelmaking was in its heyday would have made sense if the efficiency of their old equipment was high enough to enable these firms to keep pace with their better-equipped foreign competitors. This, however, was not the case. Whereas labor productivity in British steelworks and rolling mills had been 50 per cent greater than in American establishments in 1860 and two-and-a-half times greater than German productivity, output per worker in German works was 80 per cent higher than in British works by 1914, and American productivity was 57 per cent higher. Total factor productivity in the British iron and steel industry in 1907–9 was 15 per cent lower than the productivity of the German and American industries (Allen 1979: 917–19).

The more rapid deployment of the Thomas–Gilchrist process, especially in new, integrated plants that embodied the best blast-furnace practices, would not have enabled Britain to retain the leading position among steel-producing countries in the decades up to 1914. A large and affluent country with abundant natural resources like the United States was destined to make more iron and steel eventually. The concentration of production on newer, more efficient facilities and the extensive use of cheap ores, however, would have enabled British iron and steel-makers to meet German competition. Had lower costs been added to the advantages that Britain already enjoyed by virtue of its lengthy supremacy in the export trade, the iron and steel industry would have retained a larger share of the home market, satisfied a greater share of the demand emanating from the Empire, and exported in larger quantities to Latin America and the Far East (Allen 1979: 935).[5]

The British iron and steel industry failed to exploit new appliances and production methods as extensively and rapidly as did its overseas competitors in the decades leading up to the First World War. Neither demand constraints, raw material costs, nor the efficiency of inherited practices warranted this neglect of innovations that others employed with profit, and the industry paid the price for its technological conservatism in declining competitiveness and lost custom. Here, in the history of an industry that supplied one of the essential ingredients of modern economic life, is clear-cut evidence of a British resistance to technological change. Did the sclerosis that afflicted iron and steel manifest itself in other industries at other times?

Cotton textiles, like iron and steel, had been at the forefront of those changes in organization and technique that defined the industrial revolution in Britain. Through the nineteenth century the industry was a pillar of the domestic economy, and, like iron and steel, a powerful force in international trade. After 1913, however, cotton entered into a "spectacular and steady decline" (Sandberg 1974: 3). Exports, which, though increasing absolutely, had fallen from 82 per cent to 58 per cent of the world's cotton trade between 1882–4 and 1910–13, now contracted, and Britain's share of the international cotton trade sank to 39 per cent in 1926–8 and 28 per cent in 1936–8.[6] The Second World War failed to halt the slide, and by the mid-1950s cotton's share of world trade was a meagre 12 per cent (ibid.: 179, Table 26). As cotton firms had long been heavily dependent on overseas sales (in 1912 86 per cent of cotton piece-goods and 70 per cent of the raw cotton consumed had gone to exports), this radical loss of overseas trade occasioned a severe contraction of the industry. Yarn production in 1934 was 40 per cent less than in 1912, and cloth output was down by 55 per cent (Lazonick 1986: 18 and 34).

In the decades immediately preceding this collapse the industry resisted innovations in spinning and weaving machinery. The ring spindle emerged in the 1870s and 1880s as an alternative to the spinning mule, "the dominant technology in the British spinning industry from the late eighteenth century," and it very rapidly came to predominate in the American cotton industry (ibid.: 19). British manufacturers of textile machinery produced rings on a large scale and did a healthy export trade in them, but few rings were sold at home (Saxonhouse and Wright 1984: 508–13). In 1913, when rings accounted for 87 per cent of all American spindles, mules still outnumbered rings in Lancashire by a factor of more than four to one. As late as 1954 more than half of all British spindles were mules (Lazonick 1986: 19–20).

The major technological departure in the weaving section of the industry was the automatic or Northrup loom. An English invention, the automatic loom was first manufactured on a commercial basis by the American firm of George Draper & Sons. No British weaving firms installed Northrup looms until after the turn of the century, and the establishment in 1904 of the British Northrup Loom Company to manufacture and market the machine did little to accelerate its diffusion. The standard Lancashire loom still accounted for 98–9 per cent of all British looms in 1914 (when 40 per cent of all looms in the New England textile industry were Northrups) and 88 per cent in 1955 (Coleman and MacLeod 1986: 589; Sandberg 1974: 68–9; and Lazonick 1986: 19–20).

Unlike their counterparts in steel who slighted the Thomas–Gilchrist process, British cotton masters were not acting irrationally when they ignored the new textile machinery. The ring frame and the automatic loom did not promise them lower costs, larger profit margins, nor a greater share of the market. The essential feature of these new appliances was that they saved skilled labor. Ring spindles allowed yarn manufacturers to substitute unskilled (predominantly female) workers for skilled adult males, while the Northrup loom reduced labor costs by increasing the number of looms to which a weaver could attend. The cotton industry in Britain, however, enjoyed access to an abundant pool of skilled labor. Consequently the gains to be derived from these skill-saving innovations were smaller than in other cotton-producing countries where skill was at a premium. In fact, when the capital costs of ring spindles and automatic looms are taken into account, the financial advantage that would have resulted from their installation in British works turns out to have been extremely modest (Sandberg 1974: chs 2–4; and Sandberg 1981: 114–16).

The disintegration of cotton's export trade and the subsequent collapse of the entire industry owed very little to the technological choices made by cotton manufacturers. The exclusion of British yarn and piece-goods from markets where protectionist devices privileged domestic producers, and the emergence of foreign manufacturers whose labor costs were low enough to enable them to monopolize their home markets and to compete successfully in export markets combined to diminish the share of world trade available to Britain.[7] Since all these other cotton industries had access to the same production methods available to Lancashire, it is unlikely that the adoption of spinning frames and automatic looms would have done much to alter Lancashire's fortunes (Sandberg 1974: chs 8 and 9).

Indeed it is arguable that had Lancashire invested more heavily in the new machinery the losses that it suffered as shifts in the international supply of cotton goods occurred would have been greater than they actually were. At least that is the implication of the American experience. Rings and Northrups rapidly eclipsed mules and power looms in the United States. Yet the almost complete adoption of these appliances failed to prevent the collapse of the New England cotton trade after the First World War – a collapse that "was if anything even more throughgoing" than that sustained in Britain (Saxonhouse and Wright 1984: 519). The resistance of British cottonmasters to technological change therefore seems to have been a matter of sound judgment, not entrepreneurial inertia (ibid. and Sandberg 1974: 205).

Automobile manufacture emerged as a new industry at the end of the nineteenth century. As the *locus classicus* of mass production it came to be the prototypical industry of the second industrial revolution. Here, in the US, in the years before the First World War, Henry Ford and his engineers elaborated those practices – standardized products and interchangeable parts; single-purpose machine tools and the use of semi-skilled labor; moving assembly lines and mechanical parts delivery – that made large-scale, low-cost production feasible. Here, in the US, in the years after the Second World War, automation – in the shape of transfer machines that moved pieces of metal from one tool to another without human intervention until the sequence of machining operations was completed – was integrated into manufacturing practice at Ford's Brook Park plant in Cleveland. The history of the car industry in Britain thus provides a prime test of Britain's responsiveness to the techniques of mass production – and a test of Britain's capacity to innovate in the absence of constraints imposed by an early start.

From the technological point of view British automotive engineering never measured up to the best American practice. Until 1914 motor car production in Britain remained rooted in the craft tradition of the nineteenth century. The product line of even the most successful manufacturers was highly diverse, and interchangeability was achieved to only a limited extent. As a result car-makers continued to rely heavily on general-purpose machine tools, and assembly involved much hand fitting and finishing (Saul 1962: 41–4; and Lewchuk 1989: 26–7).

There was, to be sure, some progress on the production front. Firms like Daimler and Humber adopted the repetition methods and the specialized machine tools that cycle-makers had employed previously, and the percentage of the unskilled in their work-forces increased. In the best shops engine production was carried out with sophisticated machinery that limited the amount of manual labor that was required. Nor were British components suppliers invariably backward, pioneering, as they did, innovations in the pressing of steel bodies and the production of chassis frames (Saul 1962: 36–7; and Lewchuk 1989: 24–7).

The overall picture of pre-war car-making, however, is one of patchy progress. Even those companies that adopted modern techniques for the production of engines continued to conduct final assembly on a craft basis that necessitated a good deal of skilled labor and much manual work. And innovative components suppliers found much greater interest in their bodies and chassis abroad than among domestic car-makers (Saul 1962: 36–7 and 41–4; and Lewchuk 1989: 26–7).

The 1920s and 1930s witnessed a tremendous expansion in the demand for private cars and commercial vehicles (on the order of 14.5 times), and the motor car manufacturers responded by introducing 'Fordist' practices into their works. Austin set up assembly lines in 1924 and rearranged the layout at Longbridge to facilitate continuous flow production. Over the next four years a large number of specialized machine tools were installed, and mechanical means of handling materials were put in place. In 1928 the assembly of chassis and car bodies was transferred to mechanically driven tracks. Some 14–15 years after Ford, Austin had given Britain its first domestically-owned, mass-production automobile factory (Church 1979: 97–100).

Morris Motors, Britain's largest car-maker from 1924, was even slower to embrace Fordism. Assembly was organized on a line basis after 1919 at Cowley where chassis were moved between work stations on wheeled carts. Interchangeability was extended more rapidly in the early 1920s than at other British car works, but the division of labor at

Morris was less highly developed than in American plants, few single-purpose machine tools were used, much grinding and shaping was still done by hand, and work-cycle times were slow. Moving assembly-lines, conveyor belts, and the mechanization of the assembly process were introduced into the Cowley works only in 1933–4, and as late as 1939 Britain's largest auto-maker still made extensive use of complicated, general-purpose machine tools (Overy 1976: 19, 54 and 86–8; Lewchuk 1987: 167–70; Church and Miller 1977: 181 and 186, note 67; and Tolliday 1987: 37–8).

After the Second World War the demand for motor vehicles accelerated rapidly, and the mass market finally arrived in Britain and on the continent. The British Motor Corporation (BMC) (formed by the amalgamation of Morris and Austin in 1952 and merged with the truck manufacturer Leyland in 1968 to form the British Leyland Motor Corporation) enlarged capacity to meet this demand but in a way that held down the costs of expansion. Instead of building new factories that embodied the increasingly capital-intensive technologies that Ford had evolved and continental volume producers like Volkswagen were now adopting, BMC and, after it, Leyland "concentrated on reorganizing and re-equipping the existing ones, incrementally adding new machines or lines alongside the old" (Tolliday 1988: 69). "Wherever possible" the heirs of Morris and Austin made do with "the duplication of existing machines and lines" (Williams, Williams, and Thomas 1983: 220). Innovation was not lacking entirely – BMC was one of two European companies to adapt automatic transfer machinery to lower volume engine production – but manufacturing methods continued to fall short of American standards. Automated equipment was introduced into welding, painting, and quality control in a slow, piecemeal fashion, and production remained labor-intensive (ibid.: 220–1; and Tolliday 1988: 69).[8]

The absence of the most advanced tools and techniques from the floors of British factories meant that car workers in Britain consistently failed to reach the productivity levels achieved by their counterparts in the American industry. The average British worker in 1935 produced 2.86 cars; the average American worker produced 8.76 cars (Overy 1976: 89). By the 1950s and 1960s BMC's workers had raised their output to 7–8 cars per year, but at the British factories of American subsidiaries and at the major European motor companies average annual output per worker now measured 10–12 cars (Williams, Williams, and Thomas 1983: 221 and 255–60).

The poor productivity of British car manufacturers did not invariably preclude success in the marketplace. Between the wars the leading

British car-makers performed quite well, raising their market shares and pocketing handsome profits. Far from diminishing their competitiveness, their labor-intensive methods were a source of strength in the market conditions of the period. The prices of automobiles in the 1920s and 1930s were still high enough to exclude all but a handful of manual workers from the ranks of car owners, and tariffs and license and petrol duties that discriminated against more powerful cars protected British producers from American competition. As a result demand was dispersed over a wide range of sizes and prices, and competition was largely a matter of design. Labor-intensive production practices, because they were better suited to the satisfaction of the requirements of comfort, style, and performance, were a distinct advantage (Church and Miller 1977: 181–3).

Nothing illustrates better the appropriateness of Morris's methods to the economic environment of the inter-war years than the fate of the Ford Motor Company in Britain. Ford had set up a Detroit-style works at Trafford Park, Manchester in 1911, and by 1914 the special-purpose machine tools and the moving assembly lines that were the *sine qua non* of genuine mass production had been installed. Able to produce in larger volume and at lower cost than any domestic manufacturer, Ford began the 1920s as Britain's leading car-maker. Content to compete almost exclusively on price, Ford began building a state-of-the-art works at Dagenham to ensure itself the most cost-efficient volume production in Britain. Instead of consolidating its lead, this strategy caused Ford to suffer a dramatic collapse. The company sold fewer cars in 1928 than in any year since 1913, even though total British sales reached an all-time high, and in 1929 its share of the market slumped to just 4 per cent. The 1930s saw a recovery in the firm's sales, but it remained in third place behind Morris and Austin, and Dagenham proved far from lucrative (ibid.: 168–73 and 180–2; and Lewchuk 1987: 152–8).

The capital-saving manufacturing methods that served British firms so well in the 1920s and 1930s and that were extended during the sellers' market of the 1950s and 1960s turned out to be poorly suited to the economic conditions of the 1970s and 1980s. After two decades when demand had outstripped supply, the market for cars became saturated from the late 1960s, and replacement buying gained precedence over first-time purchases. At the same time the liberalization of trade and the expanding export orientations of continental producers rendered markets at home and abroad more competitive. As price now assumed an important role in the sales struggles among car-makers, the poor productivity of BMC and then British Leyland took its toll.

The Austin-Morris share of the British car market fell from roughly 40 per cent in the late 1940s and 35 per cent in the late 1960s to less than 20 per cent in the 1980s. While both Ford and Vauxhall (General Motors' British subsidiary) were virtually doubling their respective shares of British car sales, output at Austin Rover (BMC's next incarnation) in 1981 was falling to little better than half its 1968 total. Once the fourth or fifth largest car-maker in the world, the company had become a minor-league producer. Exports declined absolutely and as a proportion of production, employment at the firm was cut in half, great sums of money were lost, and substantial infusions of public money were required simply to keep Britain's only domestically-owned car company afloat (Williams, Williams, and Thomas 1983: 217–18 and 276, Table 2A; and Williams, Williams, and Haslam 1987: ch. 1 and p. 125, Table B.1).

The collapse of indigenous British motor car production in recent decades cannot be attributed solely to the backwardness of manu-facturing techniques. We shall see in Chapter 5 below that marketing failures – poor design, flawed products, and inadequate distribution facilities – played a major part in the decline of the automobile industry in Britain. Even if production processes had been at the forefront of technological advance, BMC and Leyland would still have found profits elusive. Nevertheless, it cannot be denied that poor productivity was part of the British problem and that productivity was poor because of the technological choices that British managers made in the growth years of the 1950s and 1960s. In the leading industry of the second industrial revolution, as in iron and steel, one of the principal industries of the first industrial revolution, a sclerosis of technique came to afflict British manufacturing – and this despite the robust adolescence of the British automobile industry.

The histories of three of the worst cases of industrial decline confirm that British entrepreneurs have been slow to adopt innovations in tools and techniques. The automobile industry lagged behind first in the mechanization and then in the automation of assembly. Cotton persisted with mules and power looms long after rings and automatic looms were in the ascendancy across the Atlantic. Steelmakers failed to expand basic steelmaking as rapidly as their European rivals.

The failure of British enterprises to keep pace with the technological progress of their competitors did not invariably doom them to decline. The motor industry between the wars expanded output, built up an export trade, and, on the whole, operated profitably on the basis of production processes that fell short of Fordist mass production. The mules and Lancashire looms upon which cotton relied caused the industry no discernible harm before 1914. If the trade found itself in dire straits from the 1920s, a greater prior investment in the new spinning and weaving machines might well have made for an even worse situation. Even where technological backwardness did contribute to industrial decline, it was not always the whole story. The motor industry's failure to automate certainly restricted productivity growth, but fully automated plants and superior efficiency would not have resulted in a thriving British Leyland in the 1970s unless the commercial side of its operations had also been transformed.

The one unambiguous instance of a direct link between conservatism in the choice of technique and the loss of competitiveness – the late Victorian and Edwardian iron and steel industry – raises more questions than it answers. Why did British iron and steelmasters not make more extensive use of the Thomas-Gilchrist process and the innovations in blast-furnace practice when conditions were favorable to their doing so? Were they ignorant of technological advances? Were they complacent about the efficiency of their works? Or was it perhaps that they possessed the will to change but were thwarted in their ambitions by a lack of funds or the conservatism of their work-forces?

The survival of outdated production methods at best provides only part of the explanation for the decline of the British economy after 1870. Entrepreneurial resistance to technological innovation was not always unjustified, and, where it was, it is not always a sufficient explanation of decline. Even where the neglect of more efficient techniques was the principal cause of a loss of competitiveness, the question remains whether technological backwardness was the root of the problem or symptomatic of more fundamental disorders.

3   A question of skill

The injurious effect that trade unionism of the more aggressive or of the more insidious type may exercise on the trade of the country is a question of very great importance at a time when there seem to be so many difficulties in the conduct of our industries, especially in regard to the cost of production and foreign competition.

E.A. Pratt

The ignorance of the great masses of persons engaged in industry as regards natural science and technical knowledge is a bar to the progress of the individual, as well as a loss for the nation. Almost every branch of skilled labour could be developed if the persons engaged in it were trained in the elements of natural science, which come into account in the labour.

Sir William Armstrong

The efficiency of an economy depends as much on the qualities of its work people as on the tools and appliances with which they are equipped. The decline in Britain's competitiveness after 1870 therefore raises questions about the shopfloor skills of Britain's workers, the intensity of their efforts, and their dispositions towards their employers. Answers to these questions are not lacking, but they are contradictory. On the one hand, there is the paradoxical claim that the abundance of skill in Britain is ultimately to blame for the poor performance of the economy, the craft of the labor force allowing it to resist innovation, control the pace of work, and forego cooperation with the management. On the other hand, there is the allegation that British workers have been the victims of an educational system that failed to provide them with the skills needed to function efficiently in a modern industrial economy. What are we to make of these conflicting answers?

There is much to recommend the view that the British after 1870 were better suited to industrial tasks than were the populations of other lands. Britain had achieved a high degree of urbanization well in advance of the nations of continental Europe (with the exception of the Netherlands) and North America, and it had industrialized first. By the late nineteenth century most of the work-force "came from urban, industrial backgrounds and had a long tradition of industrial discipline and skills" (Harley 1974: 394–5). The habits and abilities that modern manufacturing required ought to have been more widely diffused and more deeply embedded than in countries like Germany and the United States where much of the work-force consisted of "recent immigrants to urban areas from peasant backgrounds," and there is indeed evidence that Britain was rich in skill. The labor force in both construction and steelmaking in the early twentieth century included a considerably higher proportion of skilled employees in Sheffield and Birmingham than in Pittsburgh. The differential between the wage of the skilled craftsmen and the unskilled worker was narrower in Britain than in the United States across a wide range of occupations in the decades down to the First World War (More 1980: 171–3; and Harley 1974: 395–6, 399, and 403). Skill was thus sufficiently abundant that a large pay premium was not necessary to attract it.

Easy access to a skilled work-force conferred on British employers considerable advantages over their competitors overseas. The dexterity and judgment that their employees brought to their jobs enabled manufacturers to avoid costly investment in capital equipment that substituted for human skill. The freedom of cotton spinners to persist with mules instead of installing rings is one example of this, and similar experiences can be observed in engineering and shipbuilding (Sandberg 1974: chs 2–4; Harley 1974: 398–411; and Lorenz and Wilkinson 1986: 116). The all-round ability of British craftsmen also permitted their employers to delegate to them matters of recruitment and supervision. In cotton spinning the adult male mule spinner hired his helpers and bore the responsibility for monitoring their competence and industry. His employer, in turn, was spared the expense of recruiting the unskilled employees in his works and superintending their labor (Lazonick 1979: 236–46). The availability of skilled workers willing to transmit their skills cheaply and efficiently through apprenticeships and informal on-the-job training arrangements allowed industrialists to economize on formal training programs (More 1980: 176 and 218–19). The wide diffusion of skills among British workers, in short, reduced the production costs of the manufacturers who employed them.

The benefits of a skill-rich labor force, however, were not free. By virtue of their reliance on skilled craftsmen British employers relinquished much of their authority over the production methods employed in their works, the skill requirements of these techniques, and the overall level of employment at their firms. Over time the decisions that skilled workmen made acquired the status of custom. Managerial attempts to alter them appeared as attacks on the "norm" and invited stiff resistance from craftsmen who had become habituated to a significant degree of autonomy in the workplace. The central position that skilled workers occupied in the production process – as much by virtue of their managerial skills as by their technical skills – and the relatively full employment and high wages that they enjoyed enabled them to form powerful craft unions capable of defending the shopfloor prerogatives of their members. Employers who contented themselves with production techniques dependent on skilled workers and who willingly delegated responsibility for recruitment, supervision, and training to them found themselves severely limited in their ability to determine the manufacturing methods employed in their factories, the employment requirements of their works, and the efforts of their labor force. To acquiesce to this state of affairs was to consign the firm to sub-optimal efficiency. To resist it was to court industrial unrest (Kilpatrick and Lawson 1980: 85–93).

The workplace skills that minimized British production costs thus generated restrictive practices, and what had been a competitive advantage in the nineteenth century became a principal cause of the economy's inability to compete in the twentieth – or so went the familiar argument that echoed repeatedly in cafés, bars, and leader columns through the 1960s and 1970s and into the 1980s. The belief that "it's the bloody-minded workers and their unions who have ruined British industry" has enjoyed wide currency in popular discussion of Britain's relative economic decline, and Mancur Olson's general theory of "the rise and decline of nations" has given it a measure of academic respectability (Olson 1982; Olson 1983; and Broadberry 1988: 33–4). Nevertheless, the "bad British worker" has not figured very prominently in serious writing about the "British disease". There have been few international comparisons of labor effort and performance, and most of these have relied on management to supply the relevant data – hardly a disinterested guide to the problem.[9] These studies also display a singular lack of interest in alternative explanations of Britain's poor productivity record. Consequently the responsibility of Britain's workers for the British predicament has been primarily a matter of assertion and not analysis (Nichols 1986: chs 2–4; and Nolan and Marginson 1990: 244).

In any event, there are a number of reasons to doubt that the exceptional power that British workers allegedly exercised on the shopfloor provides a satisfactory explanation of Britain's poor economic performance since 1870. First of all, the argument has limited chronological applicability. The mass unemployment that persisted in Britain throughout the interwar years – and which was concentrated in precisely those industries where skilled workers and their craft unions were most strongly entrenched – effectively undermined the capacity of craftsmen to defend established norms and customs. Similarly, there is considerable evidence that workers in Britain did not constrain the choice of production techniques in the decades preceding the slump. The engineering employers defeated the Amalgamated Society of Engineers in a major confrontation in 1897–8 and its successor, the Amalgamated Engineering Union, in another in 1922. Yet on neither occasion did they take advantage of their newly won freedom to introduce new machine tools and semi-skilled men and women into their shops to undertake "the sort of major capital investment which would have been essential for a full-scale transformation of the division of labour" (Zeitlin 1983: 38 and 48–9). In cotton the spinning firms "never undertook a united effort to change the traditional system" whereby the mule spinners each worked a single pair of mules. The spinners cooperated with their employers in improving mule-spinning technology and in increasing the effort of their helpers, and they did not resist the installation of the ring spindle at the few Lancashire firms that adopted it (Lazonick 1979: 250 and 256–7). The coal miners and their unions likewise accepted the introduction of coal-cutting machinery down the pits, concerned though they were about safety and changes in working arrangements (Campbell 1984: 41). It follows that "bloody-minded workers and their unions" can have done little to undermine Britain's competitiveness before 1950. At the most, they sustained in the post-war period a decline that had been set in motion more than half a century earlier.

How much British workers contributed to the dismal record of the economy in the 1960s and 1970s, the two decades when restrictive practices, overmanning, and strikes were perhaps most prevalent, is far from certain. Studies of the productivity- and growth-retarding effects of labor's shopfloor power during this period concentrate overwhelmingly on just two industries: newspaper printing and vehicle building (Nichols 1986: 62 and Commentary A; and Knight 1989: 369). How far their experiences, even if unambiguously supportive of the "bad worker" hypothesis, could be generalized to the economy as a whole is an open question. Newspaper printing was not a major component of the economy, and its product did not trade internationally. The industry's efficiency can hardly have borne heavily on Britain's competitiveness. Motor vehicles, of course, were a major industry in the post-war period and one that figured prominently in Britain's balance of trade. It is also an industry where the baleful consequences of an ill-disciplined and inefficient work-force are not readily apparent.

Certainly British car manufacture in the 1960s and 1970s was a troubled industry. Strikes were frequent. Management's authority over production methods, personnel deployment, manning levels, and worker effort seemed tenuous. Shop stewards attained prominence and notoriety. Labor productivity in the industry trailed behind that abroad, as we have seen, and there is some evidence connecting this with the numerous and sometimes lengthy stoppages to which the manufacturers were subjected (Knight 1989: 369). Moreover, comparative studies of British and overseas car-making facilities that attempted to control product mix, capital equipment, and the age of tools found that British production was inefficient even where machinery of similar type and vintage was used to turn out the same models (Nichols 1986: 45–50 and ch. 4).

The research that produced these unflattering findings, however, was not without its shortcomings. The analysis of physical plant, for example, disregarded the layouts of the works and the effects that differences in the use of space may have had on productivity. Nor was the competence with which British managers and their counterparts abroad arranged production, organized parts delivery, supervised quality control, superintended maintenance and repair, provided training, or conducted marketing subjected to comparative scrutiny (ibid., chs 4–5 and 8). It is therefore not possible to say how much of the deficiency found on the factory floors of British automobile companies can be laid at the door of the workers employed there. Nor is it certain that the declining competitiveness of British car-makers was primarily a matter of poor workmanship. "In 1975, when a family car cost £1,500, the total net cost penalty from using British labour was £25." The cost per vehicle of new model development, inflated by the low level of British output, was £90, "or nearly four times as large as the £25 penalty arising from bad work practices" (Williams, Williams, and Thomas 1983: 43–4).

Even if the financial consequences of poor workmanship had been more significant, we still would not be at liberty to endorse the "bad worker" hypothesis for the simple reason that responsibility for restrictive practices and industrial unrest may not have been the workers' alone. It takes two parties to make a strike, and in the 1960s and 1970s the willingness of management in the motor industry to countenance stoppages went beyond a determination to insist on its prerogative. In the context of the car-makers' commercial failings, strikes served the purpose of bringing supply into line with demand (Tolliday n.d.: 231–2). Overmanning and the closed shop were likewise consistent with managerial priorities and may have existed with executive approval. The former was a rational labor policy in a macroeconomic environment in which "stop–go" prevailed, and the latter may have promised stability and control of the workplace by insuring union cooperation with corporate aims and by eliciting worker self-discipline (Nichols 1986: 139 and 253–4; and Hyman and Elger 1981: 119 and 144).

If car-workers and their unions can be saddled with only a limited responsibility for the difficulties of an industry that came to be synonymous with workplace anarchy in Britain, the "bad worker" hypothesis has even less applicability to the other British industries that proved uncompetitive in the 1960s and 1970s. K.G. Knight's study of labor productivity in the strike-prone year of 1968 produced some results that implied that "high strike frequency is associated with high labor productivity, and this effect is not, in general, offset by the adverse effects of strike duration." His "more advisable conclusion" was that "in the 1960s, with one or two exceptions, the effect of strike activity on the level of labour productivity was, broadly speaking, neutral" (Knight 1989: 370). The persistence of closed shops and other restrictive practices through years of declining market shares suggests that managements found these arrangements inconsequential, if not actually conducive, to the realization of their aims. Indeed, it is possible to read in the long-term record of British corporate thinking the conviction that manufacturing systems that relied more on machines and less on skilled men were a bad idea, even "a disease or mental deficiency" (Lewchuk 1983: 105–6).

The argument that the abundantly skilled labor force that gave British industry a comparative advantage through the late nineteenth century subsequently undermined the economy's competitiveness does not seem adequate to the task of explaining Britain's relative decline. The power of British workers to control production practices, skill requirements, and manning levels remained limited long after decline had set in, and even in those decades when shopfloor militancy and restrictive practices appear to have been most pronounced, they may have been characteristic of only a few of Britain's industries. Furthermore, overmanning, closed shops, and other arrangements seemingly inimical to productivity growth may have owed their existence as much to the strategies and preferences of British employers as to the bloody-mindedness of the workers and their shop stewards. Finally, the evidence confirming that workplace practices did more damage to British economic performance than other factors working to weaken the country's competitiveness has yet to be produced.

The weaknesses of the "bad worker" hypothesis occasion suspicions about the historical premise on which it is based: Britain's possession of a comparatively highly skilled work-force. The support for this proposition consists of the data on work-force composition and pay differentials cited at the beginning of this chapter. Not all of the available evidence is consistent with the premise – the premiums paid to skilled engineering workers in Britain in the early twentieth century were higher than those in Germany in all categories surveyed and no lower than the American premiums in half – and even if it were, it would be of doubtful relevance (Harley 1974: 395–6). That skilled workers accounted for a larger share of the work-force in Britain and enjoyed smaller differentials over the unskilled owing to their abundance would provide no justification for the inference that British workers were more skilled than their overseas counterparts. Indeed, what relevant evidence is available suggests that the opposite may well have been the case. Studies of British exports in the period 1899–1950 by Nick Crafts and Mark Thomas demonstrate that Britain's "comparative advantage lay in unskilled-labour-intensive, capital-neutral, and human-capital-scarce commodities." Where trade involved commodities whose production required considerable skill and sophisticated technology, Britain found it too difficult to compete with other industrialized countries (Crafts and Thomas 1986: 641–3; and Crafts 1989: 133–5). The performance of those industries supplying technology-intensive goods and services in the 1960s and 1970s likewise erodes confidence in the capacities of Britain's workers (see Chapter 1). Judged by comparison with the industrial economies of continental Europe, North America, and Japan, the British work-force appears to have been short of skill, and not well endowed with it, since at least the late nineteenth century.

The finding that Britain has been deficient in human skills would not have surprised the numerous critics who for more than a century now have condemned the country's educational system for its failure to turn out a work-force with the capabilities that modern industrial life demands. Already in 1868 Lyon Playfair, a chemist trained on the continent and head of the science section of Britain's Department of Science and Art, was insisting that "the crying want of this country is a higher class of education for the foremen and managers of industry."

One year later J. Russell, in his *Systematic Technical Education for the English People*, observed that "the English people do not believe in the value of technical education" (Wrigley 1986: 169; and Le Guillou 1981: 175). Since then, lamentations about British attitudes to education and facilities for schooling have formed an enduring refrain in the debate about the nation's declining economic prowess. Sixty-four years after Russell, A. Abbott could write that "it is not generally believed that technical education can play a most important part in the struggle to increase national well being." Sir Bryan Nicholson of the Manpower Services Commission, speaking in 1986, gave this argument its most trenchant expression. "We are," he concluded, "a bunch of thickies" (Sanderson 1988: 38 and 44).

Much of the criticism heaped on British schooling has derived from comparisons with Germany. The educational histories of the two countries were indeed very different. Compulsory primary education arrived in Germany more than a century earlier than in Britain, there was close articulation between primary, secondary, and higher institutions of learning there, and the state contributed very substantially to the cost of teaching and research. In Britain there was practically no coordination between the different levels of the educational system, and government financing long remained minimal. The British system, however, was not necessarily without its virtues. Its very informality may have been a source of flexibility, and on more than one occasion it displayed a capacity for adaptation and rapid expansion (Pollard 1989: ch. 3, especially pt VII; and Sanderson 1988: 39–40 and 47).

It is nevertheless doubtful whether the strengths of British education have outweighed its weaknesses. Secondary schools and colleges and universities have never received adequate support, and access to them has remained quite limited. Vocational training of a technical sort has taken a backseat to academically-oriented schooling and to general secondary education. Provision at the university level for those subjects most relevant to modern industrial realities – science and technology and economics and business administration – has regularly fallen short of that made by Britain's principal competitors.

The state assumed responsibility for secondary education in Britain only in 1902, and throughout the twentieth century this sector has failed to meet the needs of either the nation's children or its industries. Only 4 per cent of the children born to manual workers before 1910 found places in secondary schools. Owing to the decline of apprenticeship and the paucity of alternative forms of vocational and technical training the bulk of these children received no post-elementary schooling. It was estimated in 1908 that two-thirds of all state elementary school leavers received no further education, and the Thompson Committee reported that in 1914 "only 7% of the male population was receiving any sort of trade instruction" (Sanderson 1972: 277; Sanderson 1988: 42; and Le Guillou 1981: 184).

Nor did the situation improve much between the wars. Only 2–6 per cent of the children of the lower classes found their way into Britain's secondary schools, and facilities for technical education remained inadequate, junior technical schools accounting for no more than 3–4 per cent of children in 1938. In the tripartite secondary system erected under the 1944 Education Act technical schools proved to be the poor relations of the grammar schools and the secondary moderns and claimed less than 10 per cent of the secondary school population. With the switch to comprehensives, most of the existing secondary technical schools disappeared, so that in 1976 just 5.7 per cent of all British 18-year-olds obtained a non-higher technical or vocational education. The proportion so educated was nine times greater in Germany and Switzerland, almost six times higher in Denmark, three times higher in Norway, and twice as great in Greece (Sanderson 1972: 277; and Sanderson 1988: 43–5).

With secondary provision so meager, the number of Britons who attained college and university places was necessarily very small – and this was true in comparison with other industrialized countries as well as in absolute terms. In 1910–11 the proportion of the appropriate five-year cohort in higher education in Germany was more than one-third larger than the proportion in Britain, and in 1914 there were almost six times more full-time university and polytechnic students in Germany than in Britain (Pollard 1989: 196; and Aldcroft 1975: 293). Not surprisingly, it was the sons and daughters of the manual working class that found access to higher education most restricted. Just 0.5 per cent of those born before 1910 made it to university, and of the 550,000 children who left school annually in the middle 1920s, only one in a thousand continued on to university. Subsequent reforms enlarged the number of places available in institutions of higher education and widened access, but Britain still failed to match the standards set abroad. Just 4.5 per cent of the relevant age group went on to college or university in 1958–9, compared with 5 per cent in Soviet Russia, 7 per cent in France, 10 per cent in Sweden, and 20 per cent in the United States (Sanderson 1972: 276–7 and 362).

The shortcomings of British higher education appear more glaring still when we shift our focus to the provisions made for the study of science and technology and economics and business administration. A British delegation to Germany and Switzerland in 1872 found that there were more students studying "the higher branches of chemistry" and doing research at the University of Munich than in all the universities and colleges of England combined. This great disparity in the training of chemists was to persist for decades. In 1904–5 German universities were awarding some 400 doctorates or postgraduate diplomas in chemistry annually. As late as 1908 there were fewer than 300 students on fourth-year courses in *all* the faculties of applied science in British universities and technical colleges (Aldcroft 1975: 293; and Sanderson 1972: 23).

In engineering the story was similar. There were 1,433 engineering students in British universities in 1902 when the six leading *Technische Hochschulen* in Germany alone accounted for 7,130 students. By 1912 eleven German polytechnics were graduating 3,000 engineers per annum, while the total number of first-class and second-class honors degrees in England and Wales numbered 530 – and few of their recipients had had any training in research. Nor did Britain succeed in narrowing this quantitative lag in the supply of engineers between the wars. Indeed, the number of engineers that British universities graduated in the period 1925–39 was equal to half the enrollment in German technical schools in the single year 1923 (Sanderson 1972: 24 and 271; and Aldcroft 1975: 293).

After the Second World War there was a relative improvement in British provision, and by the late 1950s the percentage of an age group receiving degrees in science, engineering, and agriculture compared favorably with the proportion in Germany, France, and Sweden. The proportion of these degrees that were awarded in technological, as opposed to scientific, subjects, though, was considerably smaller in Britain. Whereas about one-third of all British science and technology graduates specialized in technological subjects, the figure was roughly half in France and the United States, and two-thirds in Germany and Canada. And right through the 1970s, as S.J. Prais has noted, British universities continued "to produce about a third fewer graduate engineers and technologists" than did Germany (Sanderson 1972: 362; and Prais 1981: 53).

Instruction in economics and industrial administration in Britain likewise fell short of that undertaken elsewhere. By the middle 1920s, when Germany's commercial *Hochschulen* were educating some 5,000 students and another 11,000 were enrolled in economics and related subjects at other institutions, there were just 1,500 university students on economics or commercial courses in all of Britain. In 1929 alone there were twelve times as many business students in Germany as graduated with economics degrees in Britain in the entire 1925–39 period (Wrigley 1986: 180; and Sanderson 1972: 271).

The persistent insufficiency of places in Britain's secondary schools, colleges, and universities and the poverty of the resources devoted to subjects of industrial relevance have meant that the British work-force, from the top to the bottom, has been less well trained that the work-forces of other industrial nations. Managers and directors, no less than shopfloor operatives, have advanced to their positions with less education than their counterparts abroad. Charlotte Erickson, in her pioneering study of British industrialists, found that only 7 per cent of the steelmasters who held managerial posts between 1875 and 1895 had had the benefit of scientific training at a university, technical school, or military academy. The proportion with technical training among later generations rose but not by much: 9 per cent of the steel manufacturers in office in the period 1905–25 and 16 per cent of those in office in 1935–47. The proportion of this last cohort with a university degree in any subject measured 31 per cent, and this was comparable with the findings of similar studies of top managers and public company directors in the 1950s. By contrast, a 1950 study of managers in large American industrial corporations found that more than 60 per cent were college graduates (Erickson 1986: 35–42). In the 1980s some 85 per cent of senior managers in the United States and Japan were degree holders, but barely one-quarter of British managers were so well qualified (Ackrill 1988: 71).

Lower down the occupational hierarchy international comparisons are no more flattering to the British. Figures from the middle and late 1970s show that 60 per cent of all German workers but only 30 per cent of all British workers had attained intermediate or vocational qualifica-tions – that is, qualifications equivalent to an apprenticeship or full secretarial training. On the other hand, two-thirds of the personnel employed in British establishments, but only one-third of all German employees, could claim no more than non-vocational school-leaving qualifications. "Since qualified personnel tend to rise to the top of the organizational pyramid," the deficiency of skills in British works must have been most acute on the shopfloor where most productive tasks were actually performed (Prais 1981: 48 and 56).

The enduring failure of the British educational system to supply an adequate number of trained people to each occupational level produced and then sustained a vicious cycle of uncompetitive products, processes, and personnel. Lacking higher education, top officials have been less attuned to innovations in products and production methods than executives abroad and less appreciative of their potential. More content with inherited product lines and manufacturing routines, British managers have satisfied themselves with work-forces trained mainly on the job. Indeed, they have consistently chosen the practically-trained worker over the educated one. The Board of Education maintained in its 1908–9 *Annual Report* that "there still exists amongst the generality of employers a strong preference for the man trained from an early age in the works and a prejudice against the so-called 'college-trained man,'" and the same observation was to be made many times in later years (Musgrave 1981: 59; Le Guillou 1981: 173; and Locke 1984: 137). The employees of British works, because they received most of their training in-house, have exhibited a deep knowledge of established tools and techniques but also a deep commitment to them. They have therefore been less adaptable to innovations and perhaps more distrustful of them. From top to bottom, the training of the work-force has conspired to limit the flexibility and speed with which British enterprises have responded to competition from abroad.

There are, to be sure, scholars who resist the conclusion that the educational system has played a significant part in Britain's economic decline, Sidney Pollard and Roderick Floud foremost among them. The centerpiece of their case is the claim that British schools and training programs have turned out a supply of skilled personnel commensurate with demand (Pollard 1989: 207–8; and Floud 1982: 166–8). This presumes, of course, that British employers, themselves poorly educated, have accurately judged industry's skill requirements. Even if they have, though, it is not evident that the supply has equalled effective demand. At least since the end of the Second World War Britain has suffered a chronic shortage of skilled craftsmen. They were scarce in the 1950s and 1960s when unemployment was low (there were 20,000 vacancies for engineering craftsmen in 1961) *and* in the 1970s and 1980s when unemployment was high. In the period 1975–80 some 15–25 per cent of British employers cited the shortage of skilled labor as a constraint on their production (Sanderson 1988: 44).

Trained managers, engineers, technicians, foremen, and production workers have historically been in short supply in Britain because the country has failed to invest enough in the educational facilities necessary to produce them. In 1870, when Britain was still the unrivalled "Workshop of the World," it spent less of its GNP on education in science and technology than Germany did. Forty-four years later educational expenditure in Germany, at 2.5 per cent of GNP, was two-thirds again as great as the proportion spent in Britain. If Britain's international economic leadership reduced the need to invest in training before 1914, the relative decline of the economy thereafter and the country's slide down the league table of wealth per capita ought to have called forth a greater commitment to human capital formation. Yet, in 1980, investment in training by industry in Britain measured a mere 0.15 per cent of revenues, as against 2 per cent in Germany and 3 per cent in Japan (Pollard 1989: 155; Aldcroft 1975: 288 and 305; and M. Porter 1990: 498).

The decline since 1870 in Britain's ability to compete with the industrial economies of western Europe, North America, and the Far East has derived in part from the country's failure to build and maintain a work-force with an adequate complement of skills. This educational failure has been primarily the product of a misallocation of funds. Monies that ought to have been spent on schooling and training have gone elsewhere.

Has the failure to invest sufficiently in education been part of a wider pattern of capital misallocation in Britain? Have the British since 1870 devoted too little capital to industry, especially the newer science- and technology-based industries such as chemicals, electronics, and information-processing equipment? Have the British invested too much overseas? In short, has the decline of industrial Britain been the outcome of poor investment decisions? We take up these questions in Chapter 4.

4 The bias of capital

London is often more concerned with the course of events in Mexico than with what happens in the Midlands, and is more upset by a strike on the Canadian Pacific than by one in the Cambrian collieries.

The Economist

I have come increasingly to take the view that British industrial investment behavior has been much more of a symptom than a cause of our low growth rate.

David Stout

The decades when the competitiveness of British industry began to wane also witnessed the export of an enormous quantity of British capital. British overseas investment between 1875 and 1914 was in the order of £2–3 billion. Portfolio investment in the financial instruments of foreign governments and enterprises by itself accounted for "about £4.5 each year for every man, woman, and child in England, Scotland, and Wales" and this during a period when "national income amounted on average to less than £40 per person per year" (Davis and Huttenback 1988: 36). The annual accumulation of assets abroad represented about one-third of all British investment in the years 1870–1913. By the First World War foreign securities accounted for 48 per cent of the nominal value of all the issues traded on the London Stock Exchange and foreign assets for 33 per cent of all British wealth (Edelstein 1971: 83–4; and Edelstein 1981: 70).

The coincidence of this massive outflow of funds with the perceptible weakening of domestic manufacturing gave rise to the notion that Britain's financial institutions, by diverting capital from industry and trade at home, were responsible for the nation's economic decline. The transfer of vast funds overseas was attributed to the indifference of the City – the clearing and merchant banks, the brokerage houses, the insurance companies, and the investment trusts of London – to domestic enterprise and to the excessive caution of British investors who preferred the lower returns from low-risk investments abroad to the potentially higher rewards available through participation in ventures within Britain. This aversion to domestic business was thought to be most consequential for new industries such as electricity supply, electrical equipment, and motor vehicles, which relied on developments in science and technology and whose initial capital requirements seemed especially large.

First articulated in the late nineteenth century, the argument that investors' biases and institutional rigidities resulted in a misallocation of funds harmful to home industry and commerce has retained a powerful appeal for analysts of Britain's decline in our own day. The hypothesis has been applied most vigorously to the late Victorian and Edwardian periods, but the insufficiency of domestic capital formation has also been invoked as an explanation of Britain's poor performance since 1914 (Kennedy 1974, 1976, 1982, 1987, and 1990; Pollard 1982 and 1989; Best and Humphries 1986; and F.E. Jones 1978). In this chapter we will examine how British industry has been financed and whether it has suffered from the rigidities and biases of the financial sector. We will also consider the productivity of the investment British industry made.

British capital exports before the First World War far exceeded the foreign lending of the other industrial nations, and capital formation at home was correspondingly slower. Savings rates in Britain, the United States, and Germany all averaged 11–15 per cent of GNP in the period 1871–1913. Britain, however, devoted 4–5 per cent of GNP to acquisitions overseas, while foreign lending in Germany and the United States amounted to less than 2 per cent of GNP. As a result Britain accumulated an unmatched share of total foreign investment. In 1914 Britain, with 44 per cent of all overseas assets, had foreign holdings in excess of those of the United States, Germany, and France combined. Its domestic investment rate of 7 per cent of GNP, though, was not much more than half of the German and American rates (Pollard 1985: 489 and 492, Table 3; and Edelstein 1982: 3 and 20–5). Nevertheless, it is unlikely that British industry went short of capital or that the City failed domestic firms.

Prior to 1914 businessmen did not rely on the financial institutions of the City to fund their enterprises. Personal savings and borrowings and the resources of relatives, friends, neighbors, and participants in related trades – mobilized by local bankers, solicitors, stockbrokers, and accountants – enabled new ventures to get off the ground.

Supplemented by ploughed-back profits, trade credits, mortgages, and overdrafts, they financed company growth. The capital requirements of most industrial and commercial endeavors were small and divisible, and these informal financial networks were sufficient for the bulk of their needs. Retained profits alone were the "single most important source of finance in the nineteenth century" in Britain, "providing approximately half the additions to capital in industrial concerns by the First World War" (Michie 1987: 101). Together with the other private sources of business finance they accounted for three-quarters of capital formation in 1856 and for two-thirds of a much larger total in 1913 (ibid.: 110 and 112; Michie 1988: 494–501; and Thomas 1978: 6–7).[10]

The London and provincial stock exchanges were not entirely divorced from the financing of industrial and commercial activity in Britain, but their role was primarily an indirect one. Their main function was to provide a secondary market where shares that had already been issued could be traded. They thus ensured the marketability of investments made privately. This promise of liquidity enlarged the pool of investors willing to participate in domestic enterprise (including commercial banks which could not make long-term loans for the purpose of capital development but which would accept securities as collateral for loans to brokers, jobbers, and investors), increased the sum of available capital, and lowered the cost of funds for home industry and commerce (Michie 1987: ch. 4; and Michie 1990: 107–10).

This symbiotic arrangement between informal and formal financial intermediaries appears to have served British industry and trade well in the fifty years before the First World War. The number of investors in domestic joint-stock companies other than railways and utilities multiplied tenfold to 500,000 between 1860 and 1910, and the capital available to domestic commerce and manufacturing through the formal financial market increased substantially: the long-term shares of domestic, non-railway concerns rose between 1870 and 1913 from 4 per cent to 19 per cent of all the outstanding securities held in Britain (Michie 1987: 119; and Edelstein 1971: 84). Nor did the new science- and technology-based industries suffer the neglect of British investors. In 1880–2 alone, 142 electrical supply and equipment companies, with a paid-up capital estimated at £23 million, were established, and by 1913–14 the electricity supply industry by itself had mobilized £66.5 million. Motor car manufacturers – whose capital needs were quite limited in the days before Henry Ford – raised £2.7 million by public flotation in 1905–7 and another £1.3 million in 1911–13 (Michie 1988: 509–10 and 524). Finally, Britain's arrangements for eliciting the nation's savings succeeded in overcoming whatever unreasonable aversion British investors may have had toward domestic enterprise. In 1882 a "firm purporting to exploit the recent advances in the generation and use of electricity" was able to issue financial instruments "worth more than the ensemble of capital goods the putative firm proposed to employ" (Kennedy 1990: 31). Fourteen years later the promoter Harry J. Lawson was able to convince 550 investors to subscribe £100,000 in equity shares in the Daimler Motor Company even though the country had not yet seen the commercial production of even a single automobile. Indeed, the failure of more than half the British makes of car by 1913 did not deter investors from putting more than £4 million at the disposal of the manufacturers (Saul 1962: 31; and Michie 1988: 524).

Funds flowed out of Britain at prodigious rates in the late Victorian and Edwardian periods because the country was increasingly wealthy (by 1905–9, foreign investments alone were generating more than £700 million per year), old reliable investment outlets such as land and consols were yielding diminishing returns, and there was a rapidly growing volume of promising overseas ventures seeking financing in London (Pollard 1985: 493, Table 4; Armstrong 1990: 119–23; and Michie 1987: 122). The retrospective calculation of risk-adjusted rates of return is an uncertain affair, but there is evidence that foreign investments brought larger returns to British investors than contemporary domestic issues and without a significantly higher degree of risk (Edelstein 1976: 321; and Edelstein 1981: 78–81; and, more ambiguously, Davis and Huttenback 1988: 83–7). Those Britons who collectively accumulated such a substantial portfolio of wealth overseas through the City of London did so in the absence of any irrational prejudice against British industry or institutional rigidity detrimental to domestic enterprise. Moreover, their actions did not starve industry and trade at home of vital capital. Informal methods of raising funds satisfied the modest requirements of most domestic ventures, including those associated with electricity and the internal-combustion engine, while the stock exchanges provided a rapidly growing quantity of capital. Where individual public issues failed to meet with a satisfactory response, as was inevitable in any capital market, private arrangements often proved satisfactory "second-best" solutions (Harrison 1981: 179–84 and 186).

That the British financial system failed the domestic economy during the two decades of mass unemployment between the wars seems no more tenable a proposition. The disruption of the international economy after the war of 1914–18 sharply curtailed the scope for profitable overseas activity. Economic and political instability abroad reduced the attractiveness of foreign investment, and the exigencies of domestic economic management brought government controls on foreign borrowing in London. The emergence of Wall Street as a major financial center during the war increased the competition for what promising foreign issues there were afterwards and reduced the profits from them. At the same time, the stagnation of international trade deprived many City intermediaries of the lucrative deals they had previously done financing exports and imports. From the conclusion of the hostilities in 1918 merchant banks and investment trusts that had once devoted themselves almost entirely to activities overseas turned increasing attention and resources to the financing of domestic enterprise. Such eminent establishments as Rothchilds, Baring Brothers, Morgan, Grenfell, Lazards, and Kleinwort, Sons & Co. concerned themselves with the issue of domestic, non-governmental securities during the 1920s and 1930s, while Britain's clearing banks were extending ever larger facilities to manufacturers and traders at home (Ross 1990: 58–65; Diaper 1990: especially 71–3; Armstrong 1990: 132–3; and Cassis 1990b: 145–9).

The result was a quickening of the flow of funds through the formal capital market to British industry and commerce. The value of manufacturing and commercial securities quoted on British stock exchanges increased by more than £900 million (that is, by more than 103 per cent) between 1913 and 1933, and most of this money went to firms operating in Britain. As a proportion of all domestic, non-governmental securities, these shares rose by 44 per cent to 39 per cent. British manufacturers and merchants certainly suffered financial problems in the 1920s and 1930s, but these originated in the poor profitability born of high costs and depressed markets – and not with the financial institutions available to serve business nor the savers who channeled capital through them (Michie 1990: 98, Table 2, 104, Table 4, 105–6, and 112).

Britain's investment history after the Second World War presents a sharp contrast to that of the period 1870–1939. The pace of capital formation from the 1950s through the 1970s was unprecedentedly rapid, gross fixed investment increasing at an annual rate that was more than twice as fast as before the First World War and in the 1920s and 1930s. This rate of accumulation, though, appears much less impressive when compared with the rates that obtained in the industrial economies of Japan and western Europe. Gross investment as a proportion of GNP was 15–30 per cent lower in Britain than in Germany, Italy, and France between 1953 and 1960, and through the 1960s and 1970s Britain's gross investment rate was consistently 8–15 per cent below the average for the OECD as a whole (Phelps Brown 1977: 4; Pollard 1982: 26, Table 2.3; and House of Lords 1985: 23, Table 3.2). When replacement investment is left to the side and account taken of additions to capital stock only, Britain's investment deficiency proves greater still. The net investment ratio in Britain for the period 1953–60 was some 40 per cent lower than the German and Italian rates for all industry and 45–9 per cent lower for manufacturing alone. This disparity in net investment rates persisted through the next two decades, so that by the middle 1970s the average British worker had much less in the way of tools, plant, and transport to hand than his counterparts in other industrial countries. According to one estimate, total assets per employee in manufacturing in 1976 measured £7,500 in Britain, about £23,000 in Germany, and just over £30,000 in Japan (Pollard 1982: 25, Table 2.2; and F. E. Jones 1978: 8).

The blame for Britain's failure to invest at rates comparable to those of most other advanced economies in recent decades has attached more to the state than the City.[11] Analysts have repeatedly concluded that the volume of funds available has been equal to the requirements of domestic enterprise but that government policies have undermined its productive employment. The growth of the public sector and the increases in tax revenues necessary to support it are held responsible for "crowding out" private investment while "stop–go" macro-economic policies are said to have disrupted the flow of capital and made it prohibitively expensive (Crafts 1988b: 21; Brown and Sheriff 1979: 255; and F.E. Jones 1978: 13–16; for the Bacon-Eltis "crowding out" thesis also see Alford 1988: ch. 3).

These explanations for the comparatively slow growth of Britain's stock of plant and machinery are not entirely satisfactory. The public or non-market sector of the economy has indeed increased substantially since the Second World War, but its expansion has been at the cost of private consumption, not private investment (Crafts 1988a: viii–ix; and Crafts 1988b: 12–13). Nor have tax revenues in Britain accounted for a larger share of GNP than in western Europe – hardly a surprising finding given that public expenditure has claimed a rising share of resources in countries there too (Phelps Brown 1977: 9–12; and Brown and Sheriff 1979: 254).

More importantly, there is reason to believe that the quantity of investment in post-war Britain has not been the fundamental problem. The gaps in the rates of capital accumulation between Britain and France and Japan account for less than one-third of the disparities in their growth rates between 1950 and 1973. The shortfall in Britain's investment *vis-à-vis* Germany accounts for just 7 per cent of the difference between their respective growth rates. In fact, the ratio of investment to output in Germany was very similar to that in Britain through the 1960s and 1970s (Crafts 1988b: 4 and 20–1; and Crafts 1988a: xi).

A unit of German investment, however, yielded far more output than did the comparable unit of British investment. Output per capital was one-third greater in Germany than in Britain in 1964, more than 50 per cent greater in 1973, and almost three-quarters as large again in 1979 (Crafts 1988a: xi). Worse still, these figures may present an excessively flattering picture of the productivity of British investment, for the increase in GNP as a proportion of gross capital investment was lower in Germany than in any of the Group Seven countries other than Britain.[12] The productive return on investment in France and Italy was more than 50 per cent greater than in Britain and in Canada and the United States more than 60 per cent greater (*Midland Bank Review* 1976: 15).

From this perspective, Britain's low investment rates appear an effect rather than a cause of the nation's relatively poor economic performance since 1945. Since additions to capital stock yielded less additional output, British enterprises expended less capital on the expansion of the plant, equipment, and transport at their disposal. That other industrial nations enlarged their stocks more rapidly occasions no surprise. Their investment expenditures generated proportionately more products and services (Alford 1988: 38; Cairncross, Kay and Silberston 1977: 13; Crafts 1988a: xi; Crafts 1988b: 20–1; House of Lords 1985: 25; *Midland Bank Review* 1976: 10–11; Smith 1986: 197; and Thomas 1978: 336).

The inefficiency of capital formation in Britain has been attributed to a number of factors: excessive expenditure on cost-cutting and labor-saving techniques and insufficient investment in new products embodying new designs, new technology, and higher value added; too much investment in property; and too little expenditure on industries with significant growth prospects (House of Lords 1985: 25). Not all of these hypotheses have been subjected yet to rigorous comparative research, but the misallocation of resources that they suggest is consistent with the picture of British industrial decision-making that has emerged so far in this book. British firms have been slow to commit resources to the introduction of new tools and techniques, and they have been reluctant to invest in the training that would have produced managers able to appraise accurately the promise of innovations in products and processes and workers capable of smooth adaptations to changes on the shopfloor. The disappointing returns that were the inevitable result of belated and ill-considered innovations may well have discouraged further commitments to areas with large potential but correspondingly greater risk, and encouraged a retreat to the seemingly secure capital gains available from land and buildings. Effective research into new products and methods and investment adequate for their commercial development might have surmounted these tendencies, but the record of British research and development in recent decades is of a piece with Britain's overall investment history. It too is a story of money poorly spent yielding a disappointing return and ultimately leading to a slackening of expenditure.

As of 1967 Britain ranked second among the nations of the OECD in terms of total research-and-development (R&D) spending. In Britain, unlike in Japan and western Europe, the government accounted for a significant proportion (nearly 50 per cent) of R&D expenditure, and only in the United States did state-financed R&D absorb a greater proportion of gross national product. The civilian commitment to research and development was less impressive, Britain coming fourth in the OECD league table in this respect (Patel and Pavitt 1987: 72; Alford 1988: 47; and Pavitt and Soete 1980: 44).

Government spending on research and development in Britain was narrowly focused in the first three decades after the Second World War, with defense, nuclear energy, space, and civil aeronautics accounting for about two-thirds of total investment. The commercial promise of these activities was limited, and the industrial countries of western Europe devoted a much smaller share of their R&D monies to them: 48 per cent in France, 26 per cent in Germany, 24 per cent in Italy, 21 per cent in the Netherlands, and less elsewhere. On the other hand British governments spent relatively little on electronics, computers, and other manufacturing (3.6 per cent compared with 5.7 per cent in Germany, 9.2 per cent in France, and 10.3 per cent in Italy), and on basic research (20 per cent as against 24 per cent in France and 50 per cent or more in Belgium, Denmark, Germany, Italy, and the Netherlands) (Pavitt and Soete 1980: 45, Table 3.2).

Industry-financed R&D in Britain mirrored the pattern of public R&D spending. In 1962, 35 per cent of the pounds British companies allocated to R&D was lavished on aircraft, while chemicals and vehicles and machinery claimed just 12 and 10 per cent respectively. Again, the expenditure programs adopted elsewhere were very different. German firms devoted 33 per cent of their R&D funds to chemicals and 19 per cent to vehicles, and spent nothing on aircraft. For Japan the figures were 28, 13, and 0 per cent, respectively (Freeman 1979: 67, Table 3.4).

This allocation of research monies gave Britain a decided lead in the defense sectors of the world economy. Between 1963 and 1976 Britain was responsible for 16 per cent of all foreign patents issued in the United States, but for 23 per cent of the patents related to aircraft, 38 per cent of those related to guided weapons and spacecraft, and 34.5 per cent of those concerned with nuclear energy (Pavitt and Soete 1980: 44). Unfortunately, this technical superiority did not translate into economic success. For one thing, Britain's R&D expenditure was poorly matched with the pattern of world trade. In the nine largest industrial economies the export markets for vehicles and chemicals – products in whose research and development Britain invested little – were both more than three times the size of the market for aeroplanes in the early 1960s (Smith 1986: 91, Table 18). For another, the allocation of R&D spending in Britain was almost identical to that in the United States, and, in the competition for the commercial rewards available from defense and civil aeronautics, Britain, without access to a large market of its own and unable to realize economies of scale, was at a decided disadvantage. Consequently, the British R&D effort repeatedly issued in expensive failures like the Concorde and the TSR2 fighter plane (Freeman 1979: 67–9; Smith 1986: 92; and Alford 1988: 47).

As the results of R&D spending fell short of expectations, the rate of investment in R&D in Britain slowed. Privately-funded R&D, as a percentage of net output, actually declined between 1967 and 1975 in Britain – and this occurred in no other OECD country. By 1975 the staff of R&D personnel employed in manufacturing was almost 20 per cent smaller than in 1967 (Pavitt 1980: 6; and Pavitt and Soete 1980: 55–7). This absolute decline in R&D spending was subsequently halted, but the British commitment remained distinctly weaker than abroad. The average annual increase in industry-financed R&D in Britain was the slowest recorded among the ten leading industrial economies for the period 1967–83 (it was 40 per cent lower than the Swiss rate, the second slowest), and taking the growth of output into account does not change the result. By the early 1980s Britain had fallen to sixth place in the league table of total R&D spending, and eight countries now spent more on civilian R&D. With R&D spending growing comparatively slowly, Britain suffered a relative decline in its capacity to innovate. In 1963 British patents issued in the United States had been equal to 57 per cent of the combined French and German total. By 1985 this figure had fallen to 28 per cent (Patel and Pavitt 1987: 72–3).

Britain's unsatisfactory R&D performance in the post-war years was not just the product of an economy growing relatively slowly. Had output per capita grown as fast in Britain as it did in Japan between

1967 and 1983, and R&D expenditure increased accordingly, R&D spending in Britain still would have grown more slowly than it did in Italy, Germany, France, Sweden, and Japan (ibid.: 73). Innovative activity declined in Britain because British businessmen committed a smaller proportion of their resources to the exploration of new products and processes than their competitors overseas. This under-investment, in turn, was the legacy of prior expenditures that had been badly placed and therefore poorly compensated.

An insufficient volume of investment has contributed to the decline of British industrial prowess since 1945, though capital formation was adequate in quantity before then and not a cause of the erosion of the economy's competitiveness. This post-war deficiency in capital formation, however, resulted less from the biases of investors, the rigidities of the capital market, and the policies of post-war governments than from the misuse of investment funds by private enterprises and the correspondingly low returns from their employment. The line of causation, in other words, ran from failings in the marketplace to the quantity of investment – and these failings, and the factors conducing to them, were in evidence long before the volume of expenditure began to play a part.

We have already discussed a number of reasons why the production capabilities of British industries weakened in comparison with those of their competitors after 1870. We have yet to consider the skills with which British businesses marketed their finished products. In Chapter 5 we turn to commercial practices and examine whether they have a place in the history of Britain's industrial decline.

5 Not a nation of shopkeepers

> Britain may be a nation of shopkeepers, but they are demonstrably not very good ones.
>
> Paul Theroux

At first glance the economic history of Britain would seem to make nonsense of the notion that poor salesmanship was an important element of the "British disease." The wonders that men like Josiah Wedgwood and Matthew Boulton worked in design, advertising, and distribution were central to Britain's emergence as the first industrial nation, and commercial excellence remained a distinctive feature of later periods. At the end of the nineteenth century "specialised multiple grocers like Lipton or Home and Colonial, shoe shops like Freeman Hardy and Willis, chemists like Boots (with 150 shops by 1900), tailors like Hepworths, newspaper and book stores like W.H. Smith and scores of others transformed the retailing scene" and helped make the British standard of living the highest in Europe (Wilson 1965: 190). In the 1970s, firms such as Laura Ashley and Saatchi & Saatchi continued to uphold the British reputation for outstanding design and efficient selling.

These notable marketing accomplishments, however, never sufficed to still the voices of criticism. The official reports of British diplomats and consuls before the First World War charged British industrialists and traders with a lengthy list of commercial failings. Domestic manufacturers, they alleged, continued to rely on the merchant-house system inherited from the days of iron and cotton to sell sophisticated capital equipment in industrialized countries where "more intensive and dynamic" methods of direct selling were needed (Aldcroft 1975: 296–7). In addition, British businessmen did not study the preferences of foreign consumers as closely as their overseas rivals, were less ready to adapt their products to the requirements of markets abroad, and failed to supply cheaper goods and extensive credit. They sent fewer bona fide trade representatives abroad, and those they employed tended to be ignorant of foreign languages and customs. Nor did manufacturers and their salesmen deign to do business in metric weights and measures nor to quote prices in currencies other than sterling (ibid.: 295–9; and Aldcroft and Richardson 1969: 154–9).

This picture of British commercial incompetence passed on by government officials was certainly overdrawn. Pre-war consuls were not always the most reliable observers of British commercial practices, as special investigations showed at the time, and British concerns employed "a wide range of institutional arrangements in addition to merchant houses" to sell their goods in foreign lands, "including travelling salesmen, technical representatives, agents, the managing agency system, branch sales-offices, and foreign direct investment in production facilities" (Nicholas 1984: 492–7). Acknowledgment of the errors of government officials and the variety of sales methods adopted by British concerns, though, is not proof that British marketing was competitive, and doubts have continued to find expression.

Surveying this same ground in 1985, the Select Committee on Overseas Trade of the House of Lords echoed earlier criticisms of Britain's commercial performance with uncanny accuracy. The nation's exporters, the Committee reported, "are also at a disadvantage in their knowledge of foreign languages . . . many are afraid of quoting in a local currency," and "it is said that [they] make far less use of market research that their competitors with the result that they are ill-informed about what the markets want and the ways in which they can serve them." Like the consular officials eight and nine decades earlier, the Lords urged British enterprises to attend more diligently to the commercial end of their businesses: "it is most important for British goods to regain their reputation for quality and reliability;" "prompt delivery should obviously be achieved at all times" and "an improvement in other features of delivery including after-sales service" may also be in order; and goods must be produced with greater "regard for the precise requirements of the export markets which [are] expected to take them" (House of Lords 1985: 59–60 and 65).

The possibility of a close link between British commercial performance – in the design, quality, and suitability of products; in the reliability of their delivery; in the availability, competence, and responsiveness of salespeople; and in the adequacy of advertising, after-sales service, and credit facilities – and Britain's loss of market share at home and abroad since 1870 would seen to demand close, careful, comparative studies of individual products and their markets. Yet the

marketing practices of British enterprises have attracted little systematic scholarly attention, and much of what we know about them is the
by-product of research into technological choice and industrial relations. In the pages that follow I bring this fragmentary material to bear
on the problem of British industry's declining competitiveness over the
last century, concentrating in the first instance on the trades that have
historically been the twin pillars of British manufacturing: engineering
and textiles.

Metal-working and appliance-fabrication provided much of the
impetus for British economic growth after 1870, and after the Second
World War the engineering trades were Britain's single most important
source of both industrial jobs and manufactured exports. Here, then,
was an industry whose performance was of crucial importance for the
maintenance of full employment and Britain's export balance. While
commercial successes were by no means unknown in this variegated
industry, significant marketing lapses occurred in key sectors of the
trade and through the entire period of decline.

Between 1870 and 1914 uncompetitive salesmanship cost Britain its
position as the leading exporter of agricultural machinery to the
Australian colony of Victoria, an area of rapid agricultural expansion.
In 1870–4 British farm-machinery manufacturers had the Australian
market almost entirely to themselves, claiming 93 per cent of the trade
while implements from the United States and Canada accounted for
only 2 per cent. By 1905–9 Britain's share of Victorian imports had
fallen to 14 per cent, and that of the North American countries had
increased to 54 per cent. According to the trade's historian, Britain's
loss of Australia's custom for agricultural implements to American and
Canadian manufacturers was primarily a matter of "non-price competition." North American firms such as Massey-Harris and International Harvester established "strong selling organizations in Australia" and marketed aggressively. They supplied the full range of
"major implements and machines in demand," they established warehouses stocked with machines and spare parts, and they entrusted sales
to their own agents rather than to merchant houses. They readily
tailored their machines to Victorian conditions, and they promoted
them tirelessly, displaying their wares "at literally dozens of county
agricultural shows," entering them in field trials and competitions, and
advertising their victories and technical merits in the press (McLean
1976: 455–61). British manufacturers won a share of the medals and
ribbons and sometimes resorted to direct selling and the setting up of
warehouses (Nicholas 1984: 505). Overall, though, British exporters
inclined to a passive sales policy and allowed the Americans to pursue

"market testing, product adaptation and sales promotion . . . more vigorously." As a result, North American firms were able to claim "some 80 per cent of total machinery imports by the First World War" even though the British manufactured "many of the 'new' lines in keenest demand" and produced machines of considerable technical sophistication (McLean 1976: 460–1).

The history of cutlery and edge tool exports from Sheffield to the United States presents a similar tale of commercial inefficiency and lost trade. In 1884–5 British and German makers each accounted for 49 per cent of total American cutlery imports. Thereafter tariffs prevented either country from participating in the growth of the American market, but in the competition for the trade that remained open to foreign wares (which remained stable in value) German manufacturers won hands down. By 1913–14 their share of American imports had risen to 67 per cent, and the British share had declined to 14 per cent. Once again, it was the products that British producers made available and the ways that they sold them – and not their techniques of production and their prices – that were to blame. Unlike their German (and Swiss) rivals, the Sheffield cutlers refused to modify their traditional designs to suit American tastes. Nor did they advertise heavily or tailor their packaging and distribution to the requirements of the newly emergent chain stores and mass distributors. Consequently, the British lost out at the quality end of the market, where advertising might have sustained the cachet of the Sheffield name, *and* at the cheaper end, where new designs were required. To make matters worse, Sheffield repeated these failures in third markets like Australia where there was also formidable American competition to contend with (Tweedale 1986).[13]

The failure to fit the product to the available market also afflicted the British shipbuilding industry after the Second World War – and with the same baleful results. From the late 1950s the demand for ships internationally came to be concentrated on large-size tankers and bulk carriers. Owing to a shortage of yard space, few European builders were able to compete for this trade, so most had to devote themselves to the construction of more specialized and more sophisticated vessels. Though their shares of world production declined, all of the leading shipbuilding countries on the continent were able to increase output absolutely on the basis of this marketing orientation. A similar approach proved successful in Britain. Austin and Pickersgill of Sunderland wrote off the construction of tankers and large bulk carriers and concentrated instead on the production of small-size dry-cargo ships. Convinced that the demand for traditional cargo vessels would be buoyant, Austin and Pickersgill endeavored to design an economical ship that would be simple to build, and to capture economies of scale by the serial production of essentially standard vessels. This combination of astute product choice and excellence of design served Austin and Pickersgill well. "From the late 1960s to the mid-1970s, A and P were the most consistently profitable shipbuilding company in Britain," and in 1976 "this one company secured about one-half of all new tonnage orders placed in British yards" (Williams, Williams, and Thomas 1983: 211). Britain's other shipbuilders failed to follow consistently the Austin and Pickersgill policy of sticking to the more specialized, more sophisticated portion of the market, in which European builders could hope to compete, and emphasizing quality design and construction and reliable delivery. Consequently, total British output stagnated while European production increased, and the British share of world launchings collapsed from 28 per cent in 1955 to 9 per cent in 1965 and 4 per cent in 1975 – and this despite the fact that British prices "were largely competitive with those of European yards" from the middle 1960s through the middle 1970s (ibid., especially 188–90 and 204–11).

During the 1930s Morris and Austin, the two leading British carmakers, had conducted the commercial side of their operations with great skill. In a market where design was more important than price, they had matched consumer preferences for comfort, style, and performance to a degree that enabled them to overcome the superior efficiency of Ford's production techniques. In the post-war period the successors to Austin and Morris – first at the British Motor Corporation (BMC) and then at the British Leyland Motor Corporation (BLMC) – did not sustain the habits of skillful marketing. Their distribution systems were ill-suited to the market conditions they faced, and their designs were inferior to those of their competitors. Together with the inefficient production facilities with which BMC and BLMC saddled themselves, poor salesmanship consigned the British car industry to an ever smaller portion of the market.

The mass market for cars in Europe remained a market for small cars into the 1960s. Manufacturers could increase sales, improve capacity utilization, and lower overheads per vehicle only by additional sales of small vehicles. This was best achieved by exporting to nearby western European countries, and by 1977 the French and German car industries were both selling more than 1.25 million cars to their neighbors. BLMC, by contrast, exported only one-tenth that number of vehicles to western Europe because it lacked the distribution system to do more. Neither BMC nor BLMC ever "had a dealer network in France or Germany, two of the big three national markets on the mainland." Thus, "in 1975, when 3.5 million new cars were sold in France and

Germany, BLMC managed to sell just 7,024 cars in these two markets"
(Williams, Williams, and Thomas 1983: 229–39).

The distributional facilities of Britain's only indigenous volume car
producer also hamstrung the company at home. In the early 1960s the
company-car sector emerged as the fastest-growing component of the
British automobile market, and by the early 1970s the corporate demand
for medium-size cars represented between 30 and 40 per cent of all new
car sales. To take advantage of this buoyant trade car-makers had to
secure sales outlets that could cater to the requirements of "fleet"
buyers. Ford UK responded quickly to this shift in demand, developing
its distribution network around a few large retailers who "were geared-
up to make volume sales." BLMC also rationalized its dealer network
but in a counterproductive way. It eliminated a portion of its smaller
dealers – and so reduced the company's accessibility to private buyers –
but without improving its facilities for corporate sales. Consequently, in
1974 "Austin/Morris had twice as many retailers" as Ford, "each
selling half as many cars as Ford's retail dealers" (ibid.: 232–4).

New models that proved exceptionally attractive to British and
European consumers over a lengthy period of time might have provided
the platform from which an effective dealer network could have been
built. This was the Japanese accomplishment of the 1970s. Unfortunately, design at BLMC was every bit as deficient as distribution. The
Marina, which was to compete against the Ford Cortina in the medium-
size car market, "was a mechanically compromised 'bitsa job' knocked
up by a front-wheel-drive manufacturer which lacked the basic product
building blocks for a rear-wheel-drive 1500/1600cc car." The Allegro,
which was to replace the ageing 1100 and stem imports of superminis
from the continent, "was a mechanically uncouth styling disaster," a
"piggy little saloon [that] could never sell against chic and functional
hatchbacks like the Renault 5 and the VW Golf" (ibid.: 238–40).

The commercial inefficiency of the British Leyland Motor Corporation was especially consequential because in 1968 BLMC was
"Britain's largest single employer and Britain's largest single exporter" (ibid.: 218). While the losses of jobs and foreign earnings
occasioned by BLMC's uncompetitive marketing were perhaps unique
in size, the phenomenon of poor salesmanship was not without
precedent in the history of British engineering. Similar problems of
product design and distribution had plagued farm machinery and
cutlery before the First World War and shipbuilding from the 1950s –
and these too had cost the country sales, employment, and income.

Cotton textiles had occupied a position in the British economy akin
to that of the motor industry in the 1950s and 1960s from the industrial

revolution to the inter-war period, when competition from low-wage producers equipped with high-quality British technology caused the industry's share of the world cotton trade to collapse from 58 per cent in 1910–13 to 39 per cent in 1926–8 and 28 per cent in 1936–8. Cotton's decline resumed after the Second World War, with its export share falling to 12 per cent in the middle 1950s and less that 3 per cent in the late 1960s, and imports taking a growing share of the domestic market (Singleton 1986: 96–101). In this later phase of cotton's demise, Lancashire was displaced from high-quality, high-price markets as well as from low-quality, low-price markets, and by high-cost producers who enjoyed no wage-rate advantage over the British. British designs and distribution facilities now proved as uncompetitive as British prices had between the wars.

Already in the late 1920s and 1930s the British cotton industry was losing out in affluent export markets to the cotton trades of other industrial economies that offered more stylish products and more attractive packaging. On a visit to Canada in 1931, Raymond Streat, secretary of the Manchester Chamber of Commerce, sought to learn why Lancashire's trade there was on the wane. He discovered that the old-fashioned nature of British goods and their prosaic display were the reasons.

> I drew Burton [president of the second largest store in Toronto] on to Cotton Goods. He said purchases from England declined some years ago because we did not keep abreast of changing tastes. They bought sheetings and pillow cases from the U.S.A. because a taste grew up for coloured goods and less heavily finished goods, neither of which were on offer from Manchester. As regards towels, the U.S.A. got away with the trade by packing in attractive forms and new designs. Underwear, particularly for men, was differently designed and made of different materials.
>
> (Dupree 1987: vol. I, 63)

After the Second World War this inability to match the design and distribution skills of cotton manufacturers in other advanced industrial economies weighed more heavily still upon Lancashire's fortunes. Two-thirds of the 51 per cent decline in British cotton exports between 1935–7 and 1949–54 occurred in expanding markets and "was caused by the substitution of exports from Western Europe and the United States" (Vitkovich 1955: 254–5). Price differentials among these producers were not consistently to Britain's disadvantage, and, where they were, neither were they great nor beyond the industry's capacity to meet them. Rather it was the speed and reliability of delivery from western European and American manufacturers and their deliberate cultivation of foreign markets that made the difference (ibid.: 254–5 and 259–65). Similar factors were at work in Britain's domestic market. Imports of finished cloth increased rapidly as a proportion of total imports between 1954–5 and 1963–4, and it was cotton producers from the EEC countries that accounted for the bulk of them. Here Lancashire enjoyed a decided price advantage but failed to deliver the fashionable designs and the prompt production schedules essential to exploiting it (Vibert 1966: 317–18).

British companies in newer industries that grew rapidly in the twentieth century were no more immune to marketing inefficiencies than the producers of engineering and textile staples. In pharmaceuticals, British firms concentrated on simple refining and repackaging and on distribution through pharmacies long after American drug companies had redefined themselves as high-technology operations and shifted their sales focus toward physicians (Liebenau 1986). American manufacturers of quick and instant foods made considerable headway in the British market before 1945 because of their "ability to differentiate between products by brand advertising and selling methods which were often – but not always – superior to those of British competitors" (G. Jones 1988: 437). Nor were problems of non-price competition unknown in the service sector of the British economy. Innovations that improved service and the breadth of their facilities helped American advertising agencies to challenge their British rivals in the British market, beginning in the 1930s, and to dominate that market from the 1960s to the 1980s (West 1988: 469–72 and 488–90).[14]

To be sure, the commercial history of British industry since 1870 is not just a lengthy litany of unfashionable wares, unexciting advertising, unflattering packaging, and uncertain distribution. In addition to the Liptons, Boots, and W.H. Smiths there have been some striking marketing successes. During the 1980s British advertising agencies that assimilated American innovations and then improved the services they made possible won back the British market and took an impressive share of the American advertising business as well (West 1988: 478–83, 494–5, and 499). Back at the beginning of the century, the British bicycle industry repelled a similar American invasion by transforming a product line devoted to high-quality, high-price machines available with an array of special features into one that emphasized cheap but durable designs, and by cultivating the customer with more attractive advertising, easy-payment systems and more favorable credit terms, and speedier spare-parts delivery (Harrison 1969: 297–9). In textiles, the woolen industry showed great competitive power before the First World

War, increasing its share of British, French, and German exports from 42 to 54 per cent between 1880–4 and 1909–13. While much of its advantage derived from economies associated with the utilization of reconstituted wool on a large scale, the Yorkshire manufacturers "worked hard and successfully to create, respond to and copy fashion movements," and they adjusted "rapidly to sudden surges in demand and changes in fashion" (D.T. Jenkins and Malin 1990: 82–3).

These worthy accomplishments in the design, distribution, and delivery of British goods and services, however, have not compensated sufficiently for uncompetitive commercial performances elsewhere in the economy. Efficient marketing has either been concentrated in sectors such as retailing which have been largely immune to foreign competition, or confined to industries like bicycles and woolens which contributed little to employment and foreign trade in comparison with cotton textiles and automotive engineering. Indeed, in the most recent past, the deficiencies of British salesmanship have been extensive enough to more than wipe out cost movements in Britain's favor. Between 1960 and 1974 Britain's share of the world trade in manufactured goods declined from 15 to 8 per cent. Britain's competitiveness, calculated on a cost basis, improved by more than 11 per cent during this time. The econometric analysis of these data on export shares and price competitiveness and information on cyclical factors indicates that "the UK export share should have risen" in this period and that non-price factors alone account fully for the relative decline in Britain's share of world trade (Posner and Steer 1979: 159).

Since 1870 British businessmen in a disturbingly wide variety of important trades have been less successful than their competitors abroad in matching their products to the available markets, in cultivating potential customers, in meeting orders promptly and reliably, and in providing financing and after-sales service. As consequential as these inefficiencies have been for sales, market shares, and profits, they have to be seen as part of a larger pattern of uncompetitive behavior that has included an indifference to education and training and a lethargy in the adoption of new tools and techniques. Across the full range of business functions and in many branches of the economy, British enterprises have not kept up with firms elsewhere. Why? Has the culture that British businessmen inhabited failed to encourage industrial accomplishment? Have government policies created an economic environment inimical to entrepreneurial initiative? Chapter 6 considers whether the choices that made British industry uncompetitive were rooted in the larger social and political world of which entrepreneurs and managers were part.

6 An anti-industrial society?

The socially mobile are portrayed as uncaring; businessmen as crooks; money-making is to be despised. British television has been an integral part of the British disease.

Rupert Murdoch

The industrial interests, the interests of the humble toiler who produces wealth, have been sacrificed to all other interests. The financiers, the minor capitalists, the bankers, the merchants, the international traders, all have been admitted to a voice in the direct government of the country before any of the industrial class were admitted to its secret councils. That is a reason for decay in British industry.

Opifex and Artifex

When Rupert Murdoch blasted the anti-entrepreneurial bias of British broadcasting at the Edinburgh Festival in 1989, he was merely repeating the deep-seated and enduring conviction that British culture has been the root cause of Britain's industrial decline. The central tenet of this tradition is the belief that the British people – and especially those of the middle classes – have long been averse to industry. For them, the real Britain has been the "green and pleasant land" of the traditional British countryside. Their heroes have been those knights of the shires who have owned the broad, bucolic acres and who have devoted themselves "to the more aristocratic interests of cultivated style, the pursuits of leisure, and political service." Toward their stately homes British manufacturers have long gazed with admiration and envy. Those businessmen who could forsake industry and trade for a life of gentility have eagerly done so. Those who have been obliged to remain in business have harbored "antibusiness values" that lent "a particular 'gentry'" cast to their endeavors and undermined their "dedication to work, [their] drive for profit, and [their] readiness to strike out on new paths in its pursuit." This "gentrification of the English middle class" thus caused "a dampening of industrial energies" – and the decline in Britain's economic prowess (Wiener 1981: 13, 24, 97, and 127).

The gentrification of the British state is said to have accompanied this gentrification of the British businessman. The politicians and civil servants whose actions have shaped the economic environment in which private enterprise has functioned have been drawn from the gentry or, if of humbler birth, educated to the ideals of style, leisure, and service at a public school or one of the ancient universities. The financiers and traders of London to whom they have looked for economic expertise have likewise been imbued with an anti-industrial disposition. Industrialists themselves have been excluded from the corridors of Westminster and Whitehall, and, consequently, decision-making has exhibited an indifference, if not a hostility, toward manufacturing. As a result, British industrialists have persistently found themselves wrestling with macroeconomic policies that hampered efficiency and profitability, as well as with foreign competition (Pollard 1982: chs 4 and 7; and Pollard 1989: ch. 4, especially sections 4 and 5).

Did this anti-industrial, aristocratic code of values actually achieve such a profound cultural hegemony in industrial Britain that the competitiveness of British manufacturing was subverted after 1870 and the process of decline set in motion? A passing familiarity with British literature suffices to confirm that the gentlemanly ideal has long exercised a fascination upon the British imagination. There has, however, been a good deal more to literary Britain's engagement with industry and trade, flattering portraits of businessmen and simple indifference coexisiting with scorn and contempt (McKendrick 1986). Has a similar ambivalence toward production and profit also been characteristic of the larger British culture or was the triumph of anti-industrial sentiments more complete? Was the assimilation of British businessmen to an ethos that denigrated their talents and accomplishments really so thorough? Did their embrace of aristocratic values precipitate a "hemorrhage" of talent from industry to the land, the professions, and public service? Can the decisions to persist with old tools and techniques, to forgo the education and training of the work-force, and to make do with outdated marketing practices be traced to "canons of gentility" that weighed heavily on the minds of entrepreneurs and managers? Has an aversion to industry long permeated public decision-making and made for policies that went against manufacturers' wishes? In this final chapter we take up these troublesome questions about the social, cultural, and political origins of the "British disease."

Assertions about the cultural origins of Britain's diminished economic competitiveness after 1870 have long been in inverse proportion to empirical investigations of the society that British businessmen inhabited, so there is far from enough evidence about social, economic, and political behavior to guide us in our approach to these matters. What little there is, though, suggests that the biases of British life have not been nearly as hostile to manufacturing as the Murdochs and their academic counterparts would have us believe. Indeed, the upper and upper-middle classes of Britain which allegedly imparted an anti-industrial cast to British values were not unambiguous in their disdain for production and profit. They did, after all, send a significant number of their sons into business. More than half (54 per cent) of the men included in the A–C volume of the *Dictionary of Business Biography* (covering business leaders active in the period 1860–1980) came from families situated in the upper reaches of British society. Moreover, this flow of elite sons into manufacturing and commerce was neither limited to the offspring of wealthy businessmen nor confined to genteel pursuits like merchant banking. Sons of landowners and professionals accounted for roughly one in four of the British steel manufacturers active in the period 1865–1953, and both groups were substantially over-represented in this quintessentially heavy industry in comparison with their incidence in the population as a whole. When the children of bankers and merchants are added, the proportion of steelmasters from genteel backgrounds rises to one in three (Jeremy 1984: 8–9; and Erickson 1986: 12, Table 2, 23, Table 5, and 24, Table 6).

The public schools to which Britain's elite sent their sons to acquire the rudiments of the classical education that a life of gentility required did not invariably divert their graduates from business careers. More than one-quarter of the Rugby School cohort of 1870 entered into manufacturing and trade (one-third if one counts business careers abroad), and the same was true of the cohort of 1895–1900. Dulwich also sent a substantial minority of its pupils into business, 45 per cent of the 1870 group and 29 per cent of the 1895–1900 group. Even lofty Harrow contributed its share of graduates to industry and commerce in the late nineteenth century, with between one-quarter and one-third of its pupils taking up business careers (Rubinstein 1990: 82–3).[15] Nor is there any reason to think that these ex-public-schoolboys proved ill-suited to the conduct of business. The "systematic training in leadership qualities," the "higher level of self-confidence," and the "connections with future top-ranking politicians and bureaucrats" that an Eton or Winchester education provided might very well have conferred genuine advantages in the world of industry and trade. After all, "the *most successful* group of nineteenth-century businessmen – namely London City bankers – had by far the highest public-school attendance rate" of all classes of businessmen (Berghoff 1990: 155 and 161, emphasis in the original).

If the social status of business was high enough for a considerable number of the sons of the landed and professional classes to take up positions within it, businessmen themselves – and again those in heavy industry – were sufficiently well esteemed to provide husbands for not a few of the daughters of the landed and professional classes. Professionals and landowners together accounted for the single largest proportion of the fathers-in-law of British steel manufacturers between 1875 and 1947, their share varying from 47 per cent for the cohort in office in 1935–47 to 57 per cent and 60 per cent for the 1875–95 and 1905–25 cohorts respectively. Among the steelmasters who had themselves come from landed or professional backgrounds, only 57 per cent married women from similar families, but 74 per cent of the second-generation steel manufacturers and 78.5 per cent of those of petty-bourgeois or working-class origins found wives from families that lived from the land or on professional salaries (Erickson 1986: 45–7). Not only were steelmasters eligible, then, as husbands for upper- and upper-middle-class women, their occupational status compensated in the marriage market for the disadvantages of their births.

Given the willingness of the landed and professional classes to embrace industry as a source of jobs for their sons and spouses for their daughters, it is perhaps not surprising that British businessmen failed to ape the allegedly anti-industrial disposition of their social superiors. Industrialists and merchants, for example, long displayed an unwillingness to educate their sons at the public schools that served as the gateways to elite status in Britain. Only 47 per cent of the 234 men who served as chairmen of Britain's largest industrial concerns in the period 1900–70 attended a public school. Only 32 per cent of the cohort that held office between 1900 and 1919 had had the benefit of such a prestigious education, and this apparently marked a considerable increase in public-school matriculation among industrialists. Just 21 per cent of the men listed in the *Dictionary of Business Biography* who had been born between 1840 and 1869 had been to a public school, and only 18 per cent of the entrepreneurs active in Birmingham, Bristol, and Manchester in the period 1870–1914 were so educated (Rubinstein 1987: 196, Table 7.10; and Berghoff 1990: 156–8). The educational histories of Britain's steel manufacturers tells a similar story. Fewer than one in five of the late-nineteenth-century steelmasters had been educated at an elite secondary school, and amongst the cohort with the largest share of public schoolboys (that of 1935–47), two out of three steel-makers had not been to a public school (Erickson 1986: 33, Table 10). Even if it were true that a classical education was detrimental to a satisfactory performance in business, the public schools can have played only a subsidiary part in Britain's decline, for the fact of the matter is that few British businessmen have been subjected to this kind of schooling.

Matched with this reluctance to provide their sons with a classical education was a readiness among British businessmen to see their offspring enter industry and commerce rather than more socially rewarding occupations. The sons of partners, owners, and directors of industrial concerns constituted the single largest source of recruits to the ranks of British steel manufacturers throughout the period 1850–1950, and the single most important source of Nottingham hosiery manufacturers between 1844 and 1952. Nor do these industries appear to have been atypical. According to one national study, families in manufacturing and trade accounted for 62.5 per cent of all business leaders in Britain in the last two decades of the nineteenth century (Erickson 1986: 12, Table 2 and 93, Table 34; and James 1990: 116). The flight of businessmen's sons from industry thus looks far more like a scratch upon the body economic than a "hemorrhage" within it.

Land ownership, of course, long remained the ultimate touchstone of social status in Britain, and the nation's wealthiest businessmen certainly seem to have availed themselves of their riches to acquire acres. The overwhelming majority of business families that amassed fortunes in excess of £0.5 million in the nineteenth century bought "sizeable landed estates," the purchase coming in the heirs' generation if not in the founder's. Those who accumulated large but less princely fortunes (between (£100,000 and £250,000) were less likely to acquire large quantities of land, though a substantial minority of 15–30 per cent apparently bought estates of 2,000 acres or more (Thompson 1990: 44–5, 51–2, and Appendix I).

What consequences these acquisitions of country properties had for Britain's economic performance after 1870, however, is far from clear. The purchase of an estate did not lead inevitably to the withdrawal from business. Nor was the possession and enjoyment of landed property incompatible with continued success in industry or trade (Thompson 1990: 52–8; and Trainor 1989: 186–8). In fact, the histories of merchant families such as the Gibbs, and manufacturing families such as the Gregs, show that the purchase of land could serve the financial interests of the original concern by diversifying its assets, providing safe investments, and counteracting the trade cycle (Daunton 1989: 130–1).

It is also questionable whether the propensity of successful manufacturers and merchants to become landowners in the nineteenth century represented a new departure. Land and the status that its possession entailed had figured in the definition and distribution of prestige in Britain long before 1870. Similarly, wealth acquired in industry and trade had been devoted to the purchase of acres and esteem in Britain long before industrialization, let alone the onset of relative decline.[16] Since the purchase of estates by businessmen did not damage the economy prior to the last third of the nineteenth century, and since "there is no evidence that the sons of businessmen were *increasingly* deflected to the lifestyle of landed gentry" after 1870, it is hard to see why this tendency should have weakened Britain's competitiveness (Payne 1990: 33, emphasis in the original). Indeed, D.C. Coleman, in his justly famous article on "Gentlemen and Players," suggested that the allure of gentry status might well serve better as an explanation of Britain's economic "*success* before 1870 and well before that" than as an explanation of the economic decline of the last century (Coleman 1973: 110–11, emphasis in the original). Why wouldn't the prospect of buying status and standing with the profits of a successful business have inspired initiative and enterprise? Why wouldn't the departure of wealthy industrialists and traders for landed society have cleared the field "for a succession of thrusting, ambitious" men from lower down the social pyramid? From this perspective, the eagerness with which British businessmen sought landed estates makes the "British disease" more mysterious, not less.

In any event, the decline of industrial Britain after 1870 was a matter of the decisions about tools and techniques, education and training, and advertising and sales which the men who remained in the offices and on the shopfloors made. There is as yet virtually no direct evidence linking the choices entrepreneurs and managers made about production and marketing with the anti-industrial values to which they supposedly succumbed. If there was a "gentry cast" to their minds, which strongly influenced business decision-making, historians have found few traces of it in the records of British enterprises.

The one link between British values and enterprise management that scholars have documented connects industrial decline not with attitudes toward production and profit-making but with attitudes toward the family. British businessmen, analysts of the "British disease" have concluded with near unanimity, have typically viewed "their companies as family estates to be nurtured and passed down to their heirs rather than mere money-making machines," and their passion for continuity has placed family control rather than efficiency, profitability, or growth at the center of corporate decision-making. In practice this has seemingly meant that the founders of British concerns and their heirs have been reluctant to make what looked to them like "relatively risky investments in distant lands or in new and untested products and processes," particularly if these required additional capital in the form of new shares or long-term debt that "posed a threat to continuing family control." Similarly, British entrepreneurs have been slow "to recruit nonfamily managers and even slower to bring such salaried executives into top management." In short, the hegemony of family values in Britain has deterred businessmen from adopting the strategies most conducive to growth and from making the organizational innovations that such strategies required (Chandler 1986: 391; Chandler 1990: 335 and 390; Gourvish 1987: 26, 33, and 41; and Payne 1990: 34–5).

Familial considerations may well have exercised a heavy influence on business management in Britain, but it is by no means certain that British entrepreneurs and managers have been uniquely susceptible to the claims of kinship. If the importance accorded to family control slowed the separation of control from ownership in Britain before the First World War and the elaboration of managerial hierarchies, in comparison with their progress in the United States, the same force appears to have been at work in Germany also. According to Jurgen Kocka, "entrepreneurial corporations in which family members continued to exercise control may well have been more important in Germany before World War I than in the United States at the same time," and even though "the major growth of the managerial enterprise" occurred after 1918, "many entrepreneurial firms remained among the 100 largest" even then (Kocka 1980: 105). In Germany, though, the claims of family and the homage paid to them were obviously not inconsistent with innovations in products, processes, and marketing, with investment in education and training, nor with industrial growth.

The consideration accorded to family participation in British businesses was certainly not great enough to restrain the emergence of a corporate economy after the First World War. Already by the 1920s enough British firms had escaped the limits on growth that family control apparently entailed for industrial concentration to have reached the level prevailing in the United States. By the 1970s oligopoly was more deeply and more widely entrenched in Britain than in any other industrial economy. Indeed, in 1973 Britain could boast more giant firms (over 20,000 employees) than Germany, Japan, or France, the pervasiveness of the commitment to family ownership and control not withstanding (see Chapter 1 above).

In the influential view of Alfred D. Chandler, Jr., this supersession of the family firm by the professionally managed corporation has been more apparent than real in Britain. Many of the nation's largest corporations, he has argued, have been loose federations of family concerns, not integrated and centrally managed companies. Where authority has been centralized, the firm's owners have retained greater power over decision-making than elsewhere, managerial structures have been less well developed, and the responsibilities of managers without a significant stake in the business have been correspondingly smaller. Behind the façade of large corporations and a high degree of concentration, then, Britain remained "the bastion of family capitalism." As a result "the British economy as a whole failed to harvest many of the fruits of the Second Industrial Revolution" (Chandler 1986: 389–92; and Chandler 1990: 235–6).

In comparison with the United States, Britain may have evinced a more tenacious respect for familial considerations in the management of business enterprise. In comparison with other industrial economies, however, the British commitment to kinship and continuity looks less distinctive. While 30 of the 100 largest industrial companies in Britain "still contained significant elements of family control" in 1970, in 1969 40 per cent of the 150 largest German firms "were in the hands of a family or a single entrepreneur" (Channon 1973: 75; and James 1990: 120). If the persistence of the personal authority of the owner and an emphasis on familial continuity were incompatible with efficiency and growth, then the German economy ought not to have proved much more competitive than the British after 1870. That Germany remained at least as much of a "bastion of family capitalism" as Britain and yet exhibited considerably greater economic dynamism suggests that the enduring attachment to the family of British businessmen has not been one of the principal causes of the relative decline of industrial Britain.

A number of scholars, including Sidney Pollard, Frank Longstreth, Robert Boyce, and E.H.H. Green, believe that the anti-industrialism of British culture has worked its most insidious effects not in the private domain of enterprise management but in the public realm of policy formation. The alienation of politicians and civil servants – and the bankers and overseas traders on whom they have relied for economic advice – from manufacturing, they argue, has produced a succession of macroeconomic policies that have consistently sacrificed British industry to the interests of finance and commerce. Thus, at the end of the nineteenth century, Britain remained wedded to the gold standard when bimetallism would have enlarged the money supply and expanded the demand for British products, and in 1925 the country returned to the pre-war exchange rate for sterling even though this raised the price of British exports. Until the early 1930s and then again in the period after the Second World War Britain operated a commercial policy of free trade which opened home markets to overseas wares and subjected domestic suppliers to the full force of foreign competition, while other industrial countries took pains to insulate their domestic economies from outside pressures. From the 1950s the balance of trade and the exchange rate of the pound governed macroeconomic policy despite the fact that the management of these balances repeatedly imposed punitive rates of interest on industries in desperate need of investment (Pollard 1982: ch. 4; Pollard 1989: ch. 4; Boyce 1987: ch. 2; Longstreth 1979: and Green 1988).

By and large, British industrialists have not regarded these monetary and commercial policies as evidence of a tacit conspiracy of the state and the City against manufacturing. On the contrary, significant numbers of businessmen have embraced these ostensibly pro-City policies as beneficial to manufacturing and have helped to form the majorities that sustained them. The bimetallic enthusiasts of the 1880s and 1890s explicitly promoted their cause as that of the producer against the rentier, but the Association of British Chambers of Commerce consistently voted against the "producers" policy and by significant margins (Green 1988: 609). Though some industrialists expressed concern before April 1925 about the short-term consequences of returning to the gold standard at the pre-war parity, the pervasive belief among manufacturers that the return was an essential step toward the stabilization of international trade, on which their long-term prospects depended, overrode these doubts (Longstreth 1979: 166–8; Boyce 1987: 53; and Cassis 1990a: 14). Campaigns for the adoption of tariff protection regularly found industrialists arrayed on both sides of the issue, and it took a political crisis in the wake of an economic maelstrom to mobilize an effective majority against free trade (Marrison 1983: 163–7). Similarly, the "stop–go" regime of the post-war period and the financial pressures to which it subjected manufacturing did little to alienate businessmen from the Conservative governments that were largely responsible.

The support of Britain's industrialists for macroeconomic measures that seem to have been inimical to their material self-interest can, of course, be taken as the ultimate proof of their adoption of an anti-industrial ethos. On the other hand, is it really conceivable that businessmen bent on ascension into the gentry would willingly – and on so many occasions over so many decades – have acquiesced in policies that threatened to deprive them of the profits that were their only means of effecting this social elevation? Had free trade and the gold standard actually appeared to British businessmen to have been to the advantage of finance and commerce and to the detriment of manufacturing, the aspiration to gentility alone ought to have produced among industrialists a consensus in opposition to them.

For their part, the financial and commercial interests concentrated in London have not universally supported these supposedly pro-City policies. A number of financial and commercial houses supported bimetallism at the end of the nineteenth century, and in 1903 and again in 1930, when British trade policy hung in the balance, elements in the City came out strongly in support of tariff reform (Green 1988: 598; Daunton 1989: 149–50; Cassis 1990a: 13–14; and Williamson 1984: 119–20). Similarly, there were voices from within the financial and overseas trading communities – those of bankers among them – which spoke in the 1920s against the restoration of the pre-war exchange rate of £1 = \$4.86 (Boyce 1987: 53).

Divisions over commercial and monetary policy in modern Britain have been as much within industry and within the City as between manufacturing on the one hand and finance and trade on the other. This is because there have been differences of material self-interest among those in superficially similar lines of economic activity and because individuals in the same broad categories have interpreted both their own interests and the merits of the various policy alternatives in quite different ways. The macroeconomic priorities that have guided British governments over the last century may have failed to generate policies which rectified the uncompetitive behavior that originated in the private sector of the economy, but they cannot be attributed simply to an anti-industrial animus within the corridors of power. Rather, these priorities testify to the myriad links between Britain's island economy and international flows of capital and commodities, and to the consensus among policy-makers, financiers, merchants, *and industrialists* that solutions to the nation's economic ills had to be consistent with the maintenance of these links.[17]

Britain's relative economic decline since 1870 cannot be reduced to the inevitable corollary of a uniquely British distaste for industry. For one thing, attitudes toward manufacturing have been far from an unambiguous contempt, as the career and marriage choices of the landed and professional classes and the social behavior of industrialists show. For another, preferences that might have militated against growth, such as those that privileged family ownership and control, have been no more evident in Britain than in Germany, a rather more formidable economy. For yet another, the allegedly anti-industrial policies of successive British governments have appealed as much to manufacturers as to bankers and traders. That is not to say that social, cultural, and political factors have not been part of the "British disease". It is to say, though, that their part has been more subtle and more complicated than the invocation of an anti-industrial "spirit" allows.

Conclusion

Since 1870 the British economy has grown less rapidly than the industrial economies of western Europe, North America, and the Far East. The quantity of goods and services within the means of ordinary Britons has increased comparatively slowly, and their standard of living has deteriorated relative to the standards of living of ordinary Americans, Frenchmen, Germans, Italians, and Japanese.

The decline of industrial Britain cannot be attributed to an inadequate resource base. In fact, in recent decades Britain's inability to compete with the other industrial economies has been most evident in those sectors – the science- and research-based industries and the private services utilizing information technologies – where its stock of resources ought to have conferred a comparative advantage. Nor can Britain's failure to keep pace be ascribed to defects in the structure of the economy. The British allocation of resources among agriculture, industry, and services and within manufacturing has been virtually identical to the patterns of its competitors. Large corporations have been as prevalent in Britain as in the countries of continental Europe, North America, and the Far East, and industry has been no less concentrated.

Britain's failure has been the failure to produce and distribute an array of goods and services similar to that supplied by other industrial economies with an efficiency comparable to theirs. This uncompetitiveness in manufacturing and marketing has resulted from the decisions that Britain's entrepreneurs and managers have made within the corporate offices and on the shopfloors of British enterprises. British businessmen have long chosen to discount the economic benefits of formal, systematic education and training. They have instead insisted that the managers, supervisors, and production workers in their employ undergo a lengthy immersion in the practicalities of their works. This thorough grounding in how things are actually done has stifled consideration of how they might be done differently – and more profitably. British firms have thus been slow to introduce new manufacturing equipment and to alter production routines, and they have lagged behind in the modernization of design, distribution, and display facilities. British industry has also misjudged the value of alternative research and development programs, and the poor returns this spending has yielded have no doubt strengthened the commitment to the familiar.

Why British businessmen have preferred inherited tools and techniques to new ones, informal, practical training to systematic instruction, and established commercial practices to innovative marketing strategies, when departures of just these sorts have enabled foreign enterprises to win customers in markets around the globe and in Britain too, is far from clear. Certainly British businesses have not been at a disadvantage in the mobilization of capital. The power of British workers to control production practices has always been limited. The macroeconomic policies that British governments have operated have generally been those for which manufacturers and merchants have called. Nor has British culture been especially inhospitable to industry and trade. If business as such has not been greatly esteemed, profits made in manufacturing and commerce have been readily translatable into status and standing – and without a radical disassociation from their source.

To understand the many private-sector decisions that cumulatively undermined British competitiveness and sustained a relative decline that has now been in motion for more than a century, it will be necessary to attend far more closely than hitherto to these decisions and to those who have made them. Business historians will have to reconstruct the trains of entrepreneurial thought that culminated in the continued employment of established techniques, the persistence with inherited selling arrangements, the preference for in-house tutelage, and the misallocation of research and development spending. Cultural historians will have to re-enter imaginatively the social milieux that entrepreneurs and managers inhabited in order to discern the assumptions, biases, dispositions, and values that informed their views of the world and influenced, however obliquely, the framing of business strategies and tactics. In place of generalizations about "British" attitudes and "British" institutions, we shall require close, empirical inquiries into actual British enterprises and their decision-makers.

The decline of industrial Britain now has a long history, and so too does its interpretation. Our understanding of Britain's relative economic failure, however, remains incomplete and unsatisfactory. If we are to comprehend better this "British disease" and, more importantly, to devise effective responses to it, economic and business historians will have to trade extensively with their colleagues in social and cultural history. There is a great deal of work to be done.

Notes

1 It ought to be noted that the infant mortality rate in Britain in 1985 was lower than the rate recorded in the United States.

2 The decline in the importance of manufacturing to the British economy (in terms of both employment and output) quickened after 1970 and accelerated still further with the recession of the late 1970s and early 1980s. These developments excited fears of "de-industrialization" even though it was not clear that Britain's experience was unique in this regard.

3 Figures for the distribution of employment also demonstrate the tendency of Britain and other industrial economies to approximate to a common structure. The average share of the work-force employed in industry in fourteen of the OECD countries in 1979 was 34.5 per cent. In Britain 38.5 per cent of the work-force was involved in manufacturing – higher than in Japan, the USA, and seven other countries. Service-sector employment in Britain was only one percentage point greater than the average. Only in agriculture was a sizable difference observable: 2.5 per cent of all employment in Britain compared with a fourteen-country average of 7.5 per cent (Maddison 1982: 205).

4 "World" trade in this context refers to the trade of the leading industrial countries whose exports and imports historically have accounted for the overwhelming proportion of the international exchange of manufactured goods. These countries include Britain, the USA, France, Germany, Belgium, Italy, Sweden, Switzerland, Canada, Japan, and India.

5 Foreign consumers had become familiar with British iron and steel, accustomed to dealing in English, and adept at the use of English units of measurement in designing engineering products as a result of Britain's dominance of the export trade in basic metals. These were disadvantages that German suppliers had to overcome before they could supplant the British (Allen 1979: 914).

6 The decline in its share of the export trade aside, the cotton industry exhibited no sign of diminished vigor in the three or four decades before the First World War. Spinning and weaving capacity expanded by almost 25 per cent just between 1904 and 1914, and net profits on share capital showed "no indication of a declining trend between 1886 and 1913" (Lazonick 1986: 17; and Saxonhouse and Wright 1984: 518).

7 The United States, Germany, France, Italy, Brazil, China, India, and Russia were among the countries whose tariffs protected domestic cotton industries

and limited British imports. Japan and Italy were foremost among the cotton-producing countries that were able to compete with Britain in export markets by virtue of their low labor costs (Sandberg 1974: chs 8 and 9).

8 Ironically, the first attempt to automate the manufacture of motor cars took place in Coventry at the Hotchkiss engine works of Morris Motors in 1923 (Overy 1976: 84–5; and Lewchuk 1987: 167–70).

9 The problem of bias aside, management has not proven an adequate source of information on labor effort and performance. Many firms did not respond to the inquiries of researchers, and most of those that did could supply only impressionistic evidence. According to Pratten, the leading scholar in the field, "most companies found it difficult to quantify accurately the contributions of the individual causes of the productivity differentials" (Pratten 1977: 22; and Nichols 1986: 63).

10 Before the First World War British businessmen exhibited a decided preference for "finance through private negotiation." Eighty-eight per cent of the 3,477 new companies registered in London in 1904 and 83 per cent of the 6,542 established in 1911–13 chose private- rather than public-company status, even though this deprived them of the right to issue shares publicly and placed restrictions on the number of their shareholders and the transfer of their ownership (Kennedy 1987: 124; and Pollard 1989: 93).

11 By some measures the enlargement of the capital stock in the United States has been no more rapid than in Britain in recent years, but the volume of assets per capita was vastly larger to begin with (Brown and Sheriff 1979: 247, Table 10.9).

12 The Group Seven countries are the United States, Canada, Britain, France, Germany, Italy, and Japan.

13 In China too British engineering firms failed to cultivate potential customers with the assiduity of their German competitors (Davenport-Hines 1986a: 105–11).

14 American advertising agencies were able to establish themselves in Britain in part because of the loyalty of American multinationals in retaining their services in overseas markets (West 1988: 487 and 498).

15 The proportion of graduates entering business was smaller than the proportion of fathers in business for each cohort at all three schools. In no case, however, was the drift away from industry and trade between generations greater than 33 per cent, and in several instances it was considerably smaller (Rubinstein 1990: 82–3).

16 Historians are divided over the *extent* to which fortunes made in industry and trade made their way into land before the nineteenth century. See Thompson 1990: 51, note 24 and the literature cited there.

17 The idea that the macroeconomic policy requirements of industrialists have been very different from those of financiers and merchants rests on the dubious assumption that there was a rigid separation of their economic affairs. In fact, the ordinary requirements of their businesses brought manufacturers, bankers, and traders together and produced common economic interests. Social, civic, and political concerns multiplied their interactions and strengthened the bonds of commonality. See Daunton 1989: 132–42 and Trainor 1989 and consider the findings about occupations and careers presented in this chapter and those about the financing of industry in Chapter 4 above.

Bibliography

This bibliography lists the works on which I have relied most heavily in writing this book. As I have been concerned to capture the present state of the debate about the decline of industrial Britain, it is biased toward the literature of the 1970s and especially the 1980s. There are, of course, many fine works of older vintage. Readers who are interested in them or who desire a more comprehensive listing should consult M.W. Kirby, *The Decline of British Economic Power Since 1870* (Boston: Allen & Unwin, 1981) or Peter L. Payne, "Industrial Entrepreneurship and Management in Great Britain," in *The Cambridge Economic History of Europe*, vol. VII: *The Industrial Economies: Capital, Labour, and Enterprise*, Part I, ed. Peter Mathias and M.M. Postan (New York: Cambridge University Press, 1978).

Ackrill, Margaret (1988) "Britain's Managers and the British Economy, 1870s to the 1980s," *Oxford Review of Economic Policy* 4 (Spring), 59–73.

Aldcroft, Derek H. (ed.) (1968) *The Development of British Industry and Foreign Competition 1875–1914*, London: Allen & Unwin.

—— (1975) "Investment in and Utilisation of Manpower: Great Britain and her Rivals, 1870–1914," in Barrie M. Ratcliffe (ed.) *Great Britain and Her World 1750–1915*, Manchester: Manchester University Press, 287–307.

—— and Harry W. Richardson (1969) *The British Economy 1870–1939*, London: Macmillan.

Alford, B.W.E. (1988) *British Economic Performance 1945–1975*, London: Macmillan.

Allen, Robert C. (1979) "International Competition in Iron and Steel, 1850–1913," *Journal of Economic History*, XXXIX (December), 911–37.

—— (1981) "Entrepreneurship and Technical Progress in the Northeast Coast Pig Iron Industry: 1850–1913," *Research in Economic History*, 6, 35–71.

Armstrong, John (1990) "The Rise and Fall of the Company Promoter and the Financing of British Industry," in J.J. van Helten and Y. Cassis (eds) *Capitalism in a Mature Economy*, Aldershot: Edward Elgar, 115–38.

Batstone, Eric (1986) "Labour and Productivity," *Oxford Review of Economic Policy*, 2 (Autumn), 32–43.

Beier, A.L., David Cannadine, and James M. Rosenheim (eds) (1989) *The First Modern Society*, New York: Cambridge University Press.

Berghoff, Hartmut (1990) "Public Schools and the Decline of the British Economy 1870–1914," *Past & Present*, 129 (November), 148–67.

Best, Michael H. and Jane Humphries (1986) "The City and Industrial Decline," in Bernard Elbaum and William Lazonick (eds) *The Decline of the British Economy*, Oxford: Clarendon Press, 223–39.

Blackaby, Frank (ed.) (1979) *De-industrialisation*, London: Heinemann.

Blanchflower, David (1986) "What Effect Do Unions Have on Relative Wages in Great Britain?" *British Journal of Industrial Relations*, XXIV (July), 195–204.

Bowden, Sue (1990) "Credit Facilities and the Growth of Consumer Demand for Electrical Appliances in England in the 1930s," *Business History*, XXXII (January), 52–75.

Boyce, Gordon (1989) "The Development of the Cargo Fleet Iron Company, 1900–1914: Entrepreneurship, Costs and Structural Rigidity in the Northeast Coast Steel Industry," *Business History Review*, 63 (Winter), 839–75.

Boyce, Robert (1987) *British Capitalism at the Crossroads*, New York: Cambridge University Press.

Brito, D.L. and Jeffrey G. Williamson (1973) "Skilled Labor and Nineteenth-Century Anglo-American Managerial Behavior," *Explorations in Economic History*, 10 (Spring), 235–51.

Broadberry, Stephen (1988) "The Impact of World Wars on the Long-Run Performance of the British Economy," *Oxford Review of Economic Policy*, 4 (Spring), 25–37.

Brown, C.J.F. and T.D. Sheriff (1979) "De-industrialisation: A Background Paper," in Frank Blackaby (ed.) *De-industrialisation*, London: Heinemann, 233–62.

Buxton, Neil K. (1979) "Coalmining," in Neil K. Buxton and Derek A. Aldcroft (eds) *British Industry Between the Wars*, London: Scolar Press, 48–77.

—— and Derek H. Aldcroft (eds) (1979) *British Industry Between the Wars*, London: Scolar Press.

Byatt, I.C.R. (1968) "Electrical Products," in Derek H. Aldcroft (ed.) *The Development of British Industry and Foreign Competition 1875–1914*, London: Allen & Unwin, 238–73.

Cairncross, Alec, J.A. King, and A. Silberston (1977) "The Regeneration of Manufacturing Industry," *Midland Bank Review* (Autumn), 9–18.

Campbell, Alan (1984) "Colliery Mechanisation and the Lanarkshire Miners," *Society for the Study of Labour History Bulletin*, 49 (Autumn), 37–43.

Cassis, Youssef (1990a) "British Finance: Success and Controversy," in J.J. van Helten and Y. Cassis (eds) *Capitalism in a Mature Economy*, Aldershot: Edward Elgar, 1–22.

—— (1990b) "The Emergence of a New Financial Institution: Investment Trusts in Britain, 1870–1939," in J.J. van Helten and Y. Cassis (eds) *Capitalism in a Mature Economy*, Aldershot: Edward Elgar, 139–58.

Central Statistical Office (1980) *Social Trends 11*, London: HMSO.

—— (1982) *Social Trends 13*, London: HMSO.

—— (1988) *Social Trends 18*, London: HMSO.

Chandler, Alfred D. (1980a) "The Growth of the Transnational Industrial Firm in the United States and the United Kingdom," *Economic History Review*, 2nd series, XXIII (August), 396–410.

—— (1980b) "The United States: Seedbed of Managerial Capitalism," in

Alfred D. Chandler and Herman Daems (eds) *Managerial Hierarchies*, Cambridge, Mass.: Harvard University Press, 9–40.

—— (1986) "The Emergence of Managerial Capitalism," in Richard S. Tedlow and Richard R. John, Jr. (eds) *Managing Big Business*, Boston: Harvard Business School Press, 368–97.

—— (1990) *Scale and Scope*, Cambridge, Mass.: Belknap Press.

—— and Herman Daems (eds) (1980) *Managerial Hierarchies*, Cambridge, Mass.: Harvard University Press.

Channon, Derek F. (1973) *The Strategy and Structure of British Enterprise*, Boston: Graduate School of Business Administration, Harvard University.

Chapman, Stanley (1990) "The Decline and Rise of Textile Merchanting, 1880–1990," *Business History*, XXXII (October), 171–90.

Church, Roy (1979) *Herbert Austin*, London: Europa Publications.

—— (1982) "Markets and Marketing in the British Motor Industry before 1914, with some French Comparisons," *Journal of Transport History*, 3, 1–20.

—— and Michael Miller (1977) "The Big Three: Competition, Management, and Marketing in the British Motor Industry, 1922–1939," in Barry Supple (ed.) *Essays in British Business History*, Oxford: Clarendon Press, 163–86.

Coleman, D.C. (1973) "Gentlemen and Players," *Economic History Review*, 2nd series, XXVI (February), 92–116.

—— and Christine McLeod (1986) "Attitudes to New Techniques: British Businessmen, 1800–1950," *Economic History Review*, 2nd series, XXXIX (November), 588–611.

Collins, Bruce and Keith Robbins (eds) (1990) *British Culture and Economic Decline*, New York: St Martin's Press.

Corley, T.A.B. (1987) "Consumer Marketing in Britain, 1914–60," *Business History*, XXIX (October), 65–83.

Crafts, Nick (1988a) "The Assessment: British Economic Growth over the Long Run," *Oxford Review of Economic Policy*, 4 (Spring), i–xxi.

—— (1988b) *British Economic Growth Before and After 1979*, Centre for Economic Policy Research Discussion Paper No. 292, London: CEPR.

—— (1989) "Revealed Comparative Advantage in Manufacturing, 1899–1950," *Journal of European Economic History*, 18 (Spring), 126–37.

—— and Mark Thomas (1986) "Comparative Advantage in UK Manufacturing Trade, 1910–1935," *Economic Journal*, 96 (September), 629–45.

Crouch, Colin (ed.) (1979) *State and Economy in Contemporary Capitalism*, London: Croom Helm.

Daly, Anne (1982) "The Contribution of Education to Economic Growth in Britain: A Note on the Evidence," *National Institute Economic Review*, 101 (August), 48–56.

Daunton, M.J. (1989) "'Gentlemanly Capitalism' and British Industry 1820–1914," *Past and Present*, 122 (February), 119–58.

Davenport-Hines, R.P.T. (1986a) "The British Engineers' Association and Markets in China 1900–1930," in R.P.T. Davenport-Hines (ed.) *Markets and Bagmen*, Aldershot: Gower, 102–30.

—— (ed.) (1986b) *Markets and Bagmen*, Aldershot: Gower.

Davis, Lance, *et al.* (1972) *American Economic Growth*, New York: Harper & Row.

—— and Robert A. Huttenback (1988) *Mammon and the Pursuit of Empire*, abridged edn, New York: Cambridge University Press.

Deane, Phyllis and W.A. Cole (1967) *British Economic Growth 1688–1959*, 2nd edn, Cambridge: Cambridge University Press.

Dellheim, Charles (1985) "Notes on Industrialism and Culture in Nineteenth-Century Britain," *Notebooks in Cultural Analysis*, 2, 227–48.

Diaper, Stefanie (1990) "The Sperling Combine and the Shipbuilding Industry. Merchant Banking and Industrial Finance in the 1920s," in J.J. van Helten and Y. Cassis (eds) *Capitalism in a Mature Economy*, Aldershot: Edward Elgar, 71–94.

Dupree, Marguerite W. (ed.) (1987) *Lancashire and Whitehall: The Diary of Sir Raymond Streat*, Vol. 1: *1931–39*, Manchester: Manchester University Press.

—— (1990) "Struggling with Destiny: The Cotton Industry, Overseas Trade Policy and the Cotton Board, 1940–1959," *Business History*, XXXII (October), 106–28.

Edelstein, Michael (1971) "Rigidity and Bias in the British Capital Market, 1870–1913," in Donald N. McCloskey (ed.) *Essays on a Mature Economy*, Princeton, NJ: Princeton University Press, 83–105.

—— (1974) "The Determinants of U.K. Investment Abroad, 1870–1913: The U.S. Case," *Journal of Economic History*, XXXIV, (December), 980–1007.

—— (1976) "Realized Rates of Return on U.K. Home and Overseas Portfolio Investment in the Age of High Imperialism," *Explorations in Economic History*, 13 (July), 283–329.

—— (1981) "Foreign Investment and Empire 1860–1914," in Roderick Floud and Donald McCloskey (eds) *The Economic History of Britain since 1700*, Vol. 2: *1860 to the 1970s*, New York: Cambridge University Press, 70–98.

—— (1982) *Overseas Investment in the Age of High Imperialism*, New York: Columbia University Press.

Elbaum, Bernard (1986) "The Steel Industry before World War I," in Bernard Elbaum and William Lazonick (eds) *The Decline of the British Economy*, Oxford: Clarendon Press, 51–81.

—— and William Lazonick (eds) (1986) *The Decline of the British Economy*, Oxford: Clarendon Press.

Erickson, Charlotte, (1986) *British Industrialists*, Aldershot: Gower.

Farnie, D.A. (1990) "The Textile Machine-Making Industry and the World Market, 1870–1960," *Business History* XXXII (October), 150–70.

Feinstein, Charles (1988) "Economic Growth since 1870: Britain's Performance in International Perspective," *Oxford Review of Economic Policy*, 4 (Spring), 1–13.

Fetherston, Martin, Barry More, and John Rhodes (1977) "Manufacturing Export Shares and Cost Competitiveness of Advanced Industrial Countries," *Economic Policy Review*, 3, 62–70.

Floud, R.C. (1974) "The Adolescence of American Engineering Competition, 1860–1900," *Economic History Review*, 2nd series, XXVII (February), 57–71.

—— (1982) "Technical Education and Economic Performance: Britain 1850–1914," *Albion*, 14 (Summer), 153–71.

—— and Donald McCloskey (eds) (1981) *The Economic History of Britain since 1700*, Vol 2: *1860 to the 1970s*, New York: Cambridge University Press.

Foreman-Peck, James (1982) "The American Challenge of the Twenties: Multinationals and the European Motor Industry," *Journal of Economic History*, XLII (December), 865–81.

Fraser, W. Hamish (1981) *The Coming of the Mass Market 1850–1914*, London: Macmillan.

Freeman, C. (1979) "Technical Innovation and British Trade Performance," in Frank Blackaby (ed.) *De-industrialisation*, London: Heinemann, 56–72.

Gazeley, Ian (1989) "The Cost of Living for Urban Workers in late Victorian and Edwardian Britain," *Economic History Review*, 2nd series, XLII (May), 207–21.

Gospel, Howard F. and Craig R. Littler (eds) (1983) *Managerial Strategies and Industrial Relations*, London: Heinemann.

Gourvish, T.R. (1987) "British Business and the Transition to the Corporate Economy: Entrepreneurship and Management Structures," *Business History*, XXIX (October), 18–45.

Green, E.H.H. (1988) "Rentiers versus Producers? The Political Economy of the Bimetallic Controversy c. 1880–1898," *English Historical Review*, CIII (July), 588–612.

Habakkuk, H.J. (1967) *American and British Technology in the Nineteenth Century*, Cambridge: Cambridge University Press.

Halsey, A.H. (ed.) (1988) *British School Trends since 1900*, London: Macmillan.

Hannah, Leslie (1976a) *The Rise of the Corporate Economy*, London: Methuen.

—— (ed.) (1976b) *Management Strategy and Business Development*, London: Macmillan.

—— (1980) "Visible and Invisible Hands in Great Britain," in Alfred D. Chandler and Herman Daems (eds) *Managerial Hierarchies*, Cambridge, Mass.: Harvard University Press, 41–76.

Harley, C.K. (1974) "Skilled Labor and the Choice of Technique in Edwardian Industry," *Explorations in Economic History*, 11 (Summer), 391–414.

Harrison, A.E. (1969) "The Competitiveness of the British Cycle Industry, 1890–1914," *Economic History Review*, 2nd series, XXIII (August), 287–303.

—— (1981) "Joint-Stock Company Flotation in the Cycle, Motor-Vehicle and Related Industries, 1882–1914," *Business History*, XXIII, 165–90.

—— (1982) "F. Hopper and Co. – The Problems of Capital Supply in the Cycle Manufacturing Industry, 1891–1914," *Business History*, XXIV, 3–23.

Hatton, T.J. (1988) "Institutional Change and Wage Rigidity in the UK, 1880–1985," *Oxford Review of Economic Policy*, 4 (Spring), 74–86.

House of Lords (1985) *Report of the Select Committee on Overseas Trade*, London: HMSO.

Hyman, Richard and Tony Elger (1981) "Job Controls, the Employers Offensive and Alternative Strategies," *Capital & Class*, 15 (Autumn), 115–49.

James, Harold (1990) "The German Experience and the Myth of British Cultural Exceptionalism," in Bruce Collins and Keith Robbins (eds) *British Culture and Economic Decline*, New York: St Martin's Press, 91–128.

Jenkins, D.T. and J.C. Malin (1990) "European Competition in Woollen Cloth, 1870–1914: The Role of Shoddy," *Business History*, XXXII (October), 66–86.

Jenkins, Peter (1988) *Mrs Thatcher's Revolution*, Cambridge, Mass.: Harvard University Press.

Jeremy, David (1984) "Anatomy of the British Business Elite, 1860–1980," *Business History*, XXVI, 2–23.

Johnman, Lewis (1986) "The Large Manufacturing Companies of 1935," *Business History*, XXVIII (April), 226–45.

Jones, D.T. (1976) "Output, Employment and Labour Productivity in Europe Since 1955," *National Institute Economic Review*, 77 (August), 72–85.

Jones, F.E. (1978) "Our Manufacturing Industry – The Missing £100,000 Million," *National Westminster Bank Quarterly Review* (May), 8–17.

Jones, Geoffrey (1988) "Foreign Multinationals and British Industry Before 1945," *Economic History Review*, 2nd series, XLI (August), 429–53.

Kennedy, W.P. (1974) "Foreign Investment, Trade and Growth in the United Kingdom, 1870–1913," *Explorations in Economic History*, 11 (Summer), 415–44.

—— (1976) "Institutional Response to Economic Growth: Capital Markets in Britain to 1914," in Leslie Hannah (ed.) *Management Strategy and Business Development*, London: Methuen, 151–83.

—— (1982) "Economic Growth and Structural Change in the United Kingdom, 1870–1914," *Journal of Economic History*, XLII (March), 105–14.

—— (1987) *Industrial Structure, Capital Markets and the Origins of British Economic Decline*, New York: Cambridge University Press.

—— (1990) "Capital Markets and Industrial Structure in the Victorian Economy," in J.J. van Helten and Y. Cassis (eds) *Capitalism in a Mature Economy*, Aldershot: Edward Elgar, 23–51.

Kilpatrick, Andrew and Tony Lawson (1980) "On the Nature of Industrial Decline in the UK," *Cambridge Journal of Economics*, 4 (March), 85–102.

Kindleberger, Charles, P. and Guido di Tella (eds) (1982) *Economics in the Long View*, Vol 3: *Applications and Cases Part II*, London: Macmillan.

Knight, K.G. (1989) "Labour Productivity and Strike Activity in British Manufacturing," *British Journal of Industrial Relations*, XXVII (November), 365–74.

Kocka, Jurgen (1980) "The Rise of the Modern Industrial Enteprise in Germany," in Alfred D. Chandler and Herman Daems, (eds) *Managerial Hierarchies*, Cambridge, Massachusetts: Harvard University Press, 77–116.

Lancaster, Bill and Tony Mason (eds) (n.d.) *Life & Labour in a 20th Century City*, Coventry: Cryfield Press.

Landes, David S. (1965) "Factor Costs and Demand: Determinants of Economic Growth," *Business History*, VII, 15–33.

—— (1969) *The Unbound Prometheus*, New York: Cambridge University Press.

Lazonick, William (1979) "Industrial Relations and Technical Change," *Cambridge Journal of Economics*, 3 (September), 231–62.

—— (1981) "Factor Costs and the Diffusion of Ring Spinning in Britain Prior to World War I," *Quarterly Journal of Economics*, XCVI (February), 89–109.

—— (1983) "Industrial Organization and Technological Change: The Decline of the British Cotton Industry," *Business History Review*, LVII (Summer), 195–236.

—— (1984) "Rings and Mules in Britain: A Reply," *Quarterly Journal of Economics*, XCIX (May), 393–8.

—— (1986) "The Cotton Industry," in Bernard Elbaum and William Lazonick (eds) *The Decline of the British Economy*, Oxford: Clarendon Press, 18–50.

—— (1987) "Organization, Throughput, and Competitive Advantage: Spinning Facts and Weaving Theory," *Economic History Review*, 2nd series, XL (February), 80–6.

Le Guillou, Michael (1981) "Technical Education 1850–1914," in Gordon Roderick and Michael Stephens (eds) *Where Did We Go Wrong?*, Lewes: Falmer Press, 173–84.

Lewchuk, Wayne (1983) "Fordism and British Motor Car Employees, 1896–1932," in Howard F. Gospel and Craig R. Littler (eds) *Managerial Strategies and Industrial Relations*, London: Heinemann, 82–110.

—— (1984) "The Role of the British Government in the Spread of Scientific Management and Fordism in the Interwar Years," *Journal of Economic History*, XLIV (June), 355–61.

—— (1987) *American Technology and the British Vehicle Industry*, New York: Cambridge University Press.

—— (1989) "Fordism and the Moving Assembly Line: The British and American Experience, 1895–1930," in Nelson Lichtenstein and Stephen Meyer (eds) *On the Line*, Chicago: University of Illinois Press, 17–41.

Lichtenstein, Nelson and Stephen Meyer (eds) (1989) *On the Line*, Chicago: University of Illinois Press.

Liebenau, Jonathan (1986) "Marketing High Technology: Educating Physicians to Use Innovative Medicines," in R.P.T. Davenport-Hines (ed.) *Markets and Bagmen*, Aldershot: Gower, 82–101.

Locke, Robert R. (1984) *The End of the Practical Man*, Greenwich, Conn.: Jai Press.

Longstreth, Frank (1979) "The City, Industry and the State," in Colin Crouch (ed.) *State and Economy in Contemporary Capitalism*, London: Croom Helm, 157–90.

Lorenz, Edward and Frank Wilkinson (1986) "The Shipbuilding Industry, 1880–1965," in Bernard Elbaum and William Lazonick (eds) *The Decline of the British Economy*, Oxford: Clarendon Press, 109–34.

McCloskey, Donald N. (1968) "Productivity Change in British Pig Iron, 1870–1933," *Quarterly Journal of Economics*, LXXXII (May), 281–96.

—— (ed.) (1971) *Essays on a Mature Economy*, Princeton, NJ: Princeton University Press.

—— (1973) *Economic Maturity and Entrepreneurial Decline*, Cambridge, Mass.: Harvard University Press.

—— (1981) *Enterprise and Trade in Victorian Britain*, Boston, Mass.: Allen & Unwin.

McCraw, Thomas (ed.) (1988) *The Essential Alfred Chandler*, Boston, Mass.: Harvard Business School Press.

McKendrick, Neil (1986) "Gentlemen and Players' Revisited: The Gentlemanly Ideal, the Business Ideal and the Professional Ideal in English Literary Culture," in Neil McKendrick and R.O. Outhwaite (eds) *Business Life and Public Policy*, New York: Cambridge University Press, 98–136.

—— and R. B. Outhwaite (eds) (1986) *Business Life and Public Policy*, New York: Cambridge University Press.

McLean, I.W. (1976) "Anglo-American Engineering Competition, 1870–1914: Some Third-Market Evidence," *Economic History Review*, 2nd series, XXIX (August), 452–64.

Maddison, Angus (1982) *Phases of Capitalist Development*, New York: Oxford University Press.

—— (1989) *The World Economy in the 20th Century*, Paris: OECD.

Maizels, Alfred (1963) *Industrial Growth and World Trade*, Cambridge: Cambridge University Press.

Marrison, A.J. (1983) "Businessmen, Industries and Tariff Reform in Great Britain, 1903–1930," *Business History*, XXV, 148–78.

Mass, William and William Lazonick (1990) "The British Cotton Industry and International Competitive Advantage: The State of the Debates," *Business History*, XXXII (October), 9–65.

Matthews, R.C.O., C.H. Feinstein, and J.C. Odling-Smee (1982) *British Economic Growth 1856–1973*, Stanford, Calif.: Stanford University Press.

Maynard, Geoffrey (1989) "Britain's Economic Revival and the Balance of Payments," *Political Quarterly*, 60 (April–June), 152–63.

Metcalf, David (1989) "Water Notes Dry Up," *British Journal of Industrial Relations*, 27 (March), 1–32.

—— (1990) "Union Presence and Labour Productivity in British Manufacturing Industry," *British Journal of Industrial Relations*, 28 (July), 249–66.

Michie, R.C. (1987) *The London and New York Stock Exchanges 1850–1914*, Boston, Mass.: Allen & Unwin.

—— (1988) "The Finance of Innovation in Late Victorian and Edwardian Britain: Possibilities and Constraints," *Journal of European Economic History*, 17 (Winter), 491–530.

—— (1990) "The Stock Exchange and the British Economy, 1870–1939," in J.J. van Helten and Y. Cassis (eds) *Capitalism in a Mature Economy*, Aldershot: Edward Elgar, 95–114.

Midland Bank Review (1976) "Capital Requirements and Finance," (February), 10–17.

Mitchell, B.R. (1978) *European Historical Statistics 1750–1970*, abridged edn, New York: Columbia University Press.

—— and Phyllis Deane (1962) *Abstract of British Historical Statistics*, Cambridge: Cambridge University Press.

—— and H.G. Jones (1971) *Second Abstract of British Historical Statistics*, Cambridge: Cambridge University Press.

More, Charles (1980) *Skill and the English Working Class, 1870–1914*, London: Croom Helm.

Morgan, Nicholas and Michael Moss (1989) "'Wealthy and Titled Persons' – The Accumulation of Riches in Victorian Britain: The Case of Peter Denny," *Business History*, XXXI (July), 28–47.

Mueller, Dennis C. (ed.) (1983) *The Political Economy of Growth*, New Haven, Conn.: Yale University Press.

Munting, R. (1978) "Ransomes in Russia: An English Agricultural Engineering Company's Trade with Russia to 1917," *Economic History Review*, 2nd series, XXXI (May), 257–69.

Musgrave, P.W. (1981) "The Labour Force: Some Relevant Attitudes," in

Gordon Roderick and Michael Stephens (eds) *Where Did We Go Wrong?*, Lewes: Falmer Press, 49–65.

Nicholas, Steven J. (1984) "The Overseas Marketing Performance of British Industry, 1870–1814," *Economic History Review*, 2nd series, XXXVII (November), 489–506.

Nicholls, David (1989) "Fractions of Capital: The Aristocracy, the City and Industry in the Development of Modern British Capitalism," *Social History*, 13 (January) 71–83.

Nichols, Theo (1986) *The British Worker Question*, London: Routledge & Kegan Paul.

Nolan, Peter and Paul Marginson (1990) "Skating on Thin Ice?" *British Journal of Industrial Relations*, 28 (July), 227–47.

O'Day, Alan (ed.) (1979) *The Edwardian Age*, London: Macmillan.

Oddy, Derek J. (1970) "Working-Class Diets in Late Nineteenth-Century Britain," *Economic History Review*, 2nd series, XXIII (August), 314–23.

Offer, Avner (1983) "Empire and Social Reform: British Overseas Investment and Domestic Politics, 1908–1914," *Historical Journal*, 26 (1983), 119–38.

Ohkawa, Kazushi and Henry Rosovsky (1973) *Japanese Economic Growth*, Stanford, Calif.: Stanford University Press.

Olson, Mancur (1982) *The Rise and Decline of Nations*, New Haven, Conn.: Yale University Press.

—— (1983) "The Political Economy of Comparative Growth Rates," in Dennis C. Mueller (ed.) *The Political Economy of Growth*, New Haven: Yale University Press, 7–52.

Organisation for Economic Co-operation and Development (OECD) (1984) *United Kingdom*, Paris: OECD.

—— (1989) *United Kingdom 1988/89*, Paris: OECD.

Overy, R.J. (1976) *William Morris, Viscount Nuffield*, London: Europa Publications.

Patel, P. and K. Pavitt (1987) "The Elements of British Technological Competitiveness," *National Institute Economic Review*, 122 (November), 72–83.

Pavitt, Keith (1980a) "Introduction and Summary," in Keith Pavitt (ed.) *Technical Innovation and British Economic Performance*, London: Macmillan, 1–15.

—— (ed.) (1980b) *Technical Innovation and British Economic Performance*, London: Macmillan.

—— and Luc Soete (1980) "Innovative Activities and Export Shares: Some Comparisons Between Industries and Countries," in Keith Pavitt (ed.) *Technical Innovation and British Economic Performance*, London: Macmillan, 38–66.

Payne, P.L. (1968) "Iron and Steel Manufactures," in Derek H. Aldcroft (ed.) *The Development of British Industry and Foreign Competition 1875–1914*, London: Allen & Unwin, 71–99.

—— (1990) "Entrepreneurship and British Economic Decline," in Bruce Collins and Keith Robbins (eds) *British Culture and Economic Decline*, New York: St Martin's Press, 25–58.

Pencavel, John H. (1977) "The Distributional and Efficiency Effects of Trade Unions in Britain," *British Journal of Industrial Relations*, XV (July), 137–56.

Perkin, Harold (1978) "The Recruitment of Elites in British Society Since 1800," *Social History*, 12 (Winter), 222–34.

Phelps Brown, Sir Henry (1977) "What Is the British Predicament?" *Three Banks Review*, 116 (December), 3–29.

Pollard, Sidney (1982) *The Wasting of the British Economy*, London: Croom Helm.

—— (1985) "Capital Exports, 1870–1914: Harmful or Beneficial?" *Economic History Review*, 2nd series, XXXVIII (November), 489–514.

—— (1989) *Britain's Prime and Britain's Decline*, New York: Edward Arnold.

Porter, Andrew (1988) "The Balance Sheet of Empire, 1850–1914," *Historical Journal*, 31 (September), 685–99.

Porter, Michael (1990) *The Competitive Advantage of Nations*, New York: Free Press.

Posner, M.V. and A. Steer (1979) "Price Competitiveness and Performance of Manufacturing Industry," in Frank Blackaby (ed.) *De-industrialisation*, London: Heinemann, 141–65.

Prais, S.J. (1981) "Vocational Qualifications of the Labour Force in Britain and Germany," *National Institute Economic Review*, 98 (November), 447–59.

Pratten, C.F. (1977) "The Efficiency of British Industry," *Lloyds Bank Review*, 123 (January), 19–28.

—— and A.G. Atkinson (1976) "The Use of Manpower in British Manufacturing Industry," *Department of Employment Gazette*, 84 (June), 571–6.

Ratcliffe, Barrie M. (ed.) (1975) *Great Britain and Her World 1750–1914*, Manchester: Manchester University Press.

Roberts, Elizabeth (1977) "Working-Class Standards of Living in Barrow and Lancaster, 1890–1914," *Economic History Review*, 2nd series, XXX (May), 306–21.

Robertson, Alex J. (1990) "Lancashire and the Rise of Japan, 1910–1937," *Business History*, XXXII (October), 87–105.

Roderick, Gordon and Michael Stephens (eds) (1981) *Where Did We Go Wrong?*, Lewes: Falmer Press.

Ross, Duncan (1990) "The Clearing Banks and Industry – New Perspectives on the Inter-War Years," in J.J. van Helten and Y. Cassis (eds) *Capitalism in a Mature Economy*, Aldershot: Edward Elgar, 52–70.

Rubinstein, W.D. (1987) *Elites and the Wealthy in Modern British History*, New York: St Martin's Press.

—— (1988) "Social Class, Social Attitudes and British Business Life," *Oxford Review of Economic Policy*, 4 (Spring), 51–8.

—— (1990) "Cultural Explanations for Britain's Economic Decline: How True?" in Bruce Collins and Keith Robbins (eds) *British Culture and Economic Decline*, New York: St Martin's Press, 59–90.

Sandberg, Lars G. (1969) "American Rings and English Mules: The Role of Economic Rationality," *Quarterly Journal of Economics*, LXXXIII (February), 25–43.

—— (1974) *Lancashire in Decline*, Columbus: Ohio State University Press.

—— (1981) "The Entrepreneur and Technological Change," in Roderick Floud and Donald McCloskey (eds) *The Economic History of Britain since 1700*, Vol. 2: *1860 to the 1970s*, New York: Cambridge University Press, 99–120.

—— (1984) "The Remembrance of Things Past: Rings and Mules Revisited," *Quarterly Journal of Economics*, XCIX (May), 387–92.

Sanderson, Michael (1972) *The Universities and British Industry 1850–1970*, London: Routledge & Kegan Paul.

—— (1988) "Technical Education and Economic Decline: 1890–1980s," *Oxford Review of Economic Policy*, 4 (Spring), 38–50.

Saul, S.B. (1960) "The American Impact on British Industry 1895–1914," *Business History*, III (December), 19–38.

—— (1962) "The Motor Industry in Britain to 1914," *Business History*, V, 22–44.

Saxonhouse, Gary R. and Gavin Wright (1984) "New Evidence on the Stubborn English Mule and the Cotton Industry, 1878–1920," *Economic History Review*, 2nd series, XXXVII, (November), 507–19.

—— (1987) "Stubborn Mules and Vertical Integration: The Disappearing Constraint?" *Economic History Review*, 2nd series, XL (February), 87–94.

Shaw, Christine (1989) "British Entrepreneurs in Distribution and the Steel Industry," *Business History*, XXXI (July), 48–60.

Singleton, John (1986) "Lancashire's Last Stand: Declining Employment in the British Cotton Industry, 1950–70," *Economic History Review*, 2nd series, XXXIX (February), 92–107.

—— (1990) "Showing the White Flag: The Lancashire Cotton Industry, 1945–65," *Business History*, XXXII (October), 129–49.

Smith, Keith (1986) *The British Economic Crisis*, Harmondsworth: Penguin.

Stanworth, Philip and Anthony Giddens (eds) (1974) *Elites and Power in British Society*, New York: Cambridge University Press.

Supple, Barry (ed.) (1977) *Essays in British Business History*, Oxford: Clarendon Press.

Sutton, G.B. (1964) "The Marketing of Ready Made Footwear in the Nineteenth Century: A Study of the Firm of C & J Clark," *Business History*, VI, 93–112.

Tedlow, Richard S. and Richard R. John, Jr. (eds) (1986) *Managing Big Business*, Boston, Mass.: Harvard Business School Press.

Temin, Peter (1987) "Capital Exports, 1870–1914: An Alternative Model," *Economic History Review*, 2nd series, XL (August), 453–8.

Thomas, W.A. (1978) *The Finance of British Industry 1918–1976*, London: Methuen.

Thompson, F.M.L. (1990) "Life After Death: How Successful Nineteenth-Century Businessmen Disposed of Their Fortunes," *Economic History Review*, 2nd series, XLIII (February), 40–61.

Tolliday, Steven (1987) "Management and Labour in Britain 1896–1936," in Steven Tolliday and Jonathan Zeitlin (eds) *The Automobile Industry and its Workers*, New York: St Martin's Press, 29–56.

—— (1988) "Competition and the Workplace in the British Automobile Industry, 1945–1988," *Business and Economic History*, 2nd series, 17, 63–77.

—— (n.d.) "High Tide and After: Coventry's Engineering Workers and Shopfloor Bargaining, 1945–80," in Bill Lancaster and Tony Mason (eds) *Life & Labour in a 20th Century City*, Coventry: Cryfield Press, 204–43.

—— and Jonathan Zeitlin (eds) (1985) *Shop Floor Bargaining and the State*, New York: Cambridge University Press.

—— and Jonathan Zeitlin (eds) (1987) *The Automobile Industry and its Workers*, New York: St Martin's Press.

Toynbee, Arnold J. (1939) *A Study of History*, Vol. IV, London: Cambridge University Press.

Trainor, Richard (1989) "The Gentrification of Victorian and Edwardian Industrialists," in A.L. Beier, David Cannadine, and James M. Rosenheim (eds) *The First Modern Society*, New York: Cambridge University Press, 167–97.

Turner, John (ed.) (1984) *Businessmen and Politics*, London: Heinemann.

Tweedale, Geoffrey (1986) "English versus American Hardware: British Marketing Techniques and Business Performance in the USA in the Nineteenth and Early-Twentieth Centuries," in R.P.T. Davenport-Hines (ed.) *Markets and Bagmen*, Aldershot: Gower, 57–81.

Tyszynski, H. (1951) "World Trade in Manufactured Commodities, 1899–1950," *Manchester School of Economics and Social Studies*, XIX (September), 272–304.

van Helten, J.J. and Y. Cassis (eds) (1990) *Capitalism in a Mature Economy*, Aldershot: Edward Elgar.

Vibert, F. (1966) "Economic Problems of the Cotton Industry," *Oxford Economic Papers*, 18 (November), 313–43.

Vitkovich, B. (1955) "The U.K. Cotton Industry, 1937–54," *Journal of Industrial Economics*, III (July), 241–65.

West, Douglas (1987) "From T Square to T Plan: The London Office of the J. Walter Thompson Advertising Agency, 1919–70," *Business History*, XXIX (April), 199–217.

—— (1988) "Multinational Competition in the British Advertising Agency Business, 1936–1987," *Business History Review*, 62 (Autumn), 467–501.

Wiener, Martin J. (1981) *English Culture and the Decline of the Industrial Spirit 1850–1980*, New York: Cambridge University Press.

Williams, Karel, John Williams, and Dennis Thomas (1983) *Why Are the British Bad at Manufacturing?*, London: Routledge & Kegan Paul.

—— John Williams, and Colin Haslam (1987) *The Breakdown of Austin Rover*, Leamington Spa: Berg Publishers.

Williamson, Philip (1984) "Financiers, the Gold Standard and British Politics, 1925–1931," in John Turner (ed.) *Businessmen and Politics*, London: Heinemann, 105–29.

Wilson, Charles (1965) "Economy and Society in Late Victorian Britain," *Economic History Review*, 2nd series, XVIII (August), 183–98.

—— (1968) *Unilever 1945–1965*, London: Cassell.

Wrigley, Julia (1986) "Technical Education and Industry in the Nineteenth Century," in Bernard Elbaum and William Lazonick (eds) *The Decline of the British Economy*, Oxford: Clarendon Press, 162–88.

Zeitlin, Jonathan (1979) "Craft Control and the Division of Labour," *Cambridge Journal of Economics*, 3 (September), 263–74.

—— (1983) "The Labour Strategies of British Engineering Employers, 1890–1922," in Howard F. Gospel and Craig R. Littler (eds) *Managerial Strategies and Industrial Relations*, London: Heinemann, 25–54.

Index